THE HISTORY OF A LEGEND

JACKIE JACKSON - BAYER

BLUEROSE PUBLISHERS
India | U.K.

Copyright © Jackie Jackson – Bayer 2025

All rights reserved by author. No part of this publication may be reproduced, stored in a retrieval system or transmitted in any form or by any means, electronic, mechanical, photocopying, recording or otherwise, without the prior permission of the author. Although every precaution has been taken to verify the accuracy of the information contained herein, the publisher assumes no responsibility for any errors or omissions. No liability is assumed for damages that may result from the use of information contained within.

BlueRose Publishers takes no responsibility for any damages, losses, or liabilities that may arise from the use or misuse of the information, products, or services provided in this publication.

For permissions requests or inquiries regarding this publication,
please contact:

BLUEROSE PUBLISHERS
www.BlueRoseONE.com
info@bluerosepublishers.com
+91 8882 898 898
+4407342408967

ISBN: 978-93-7018-043-7

Cover Design: Aman Sharma
Typesetting: Pooja Sharma

First Edition: May 2025

Contents

What were your grandparents like?...1

What is one of your favorite children's stories? 5

What was life like growing up in Cochin? 7

Tell us about your Dad..18

Tell us about your Mum 26

Were your parents strict, or relaxed?......................................41

How did you meet your spouse? 44

Are you still friends with any of your friends from high school? How have they changed since then? 51

Who are your children?...57

Tell us about your brothers and sisters..................................86

What is one of your fondest childhood memories? 101

How did you get your first job? 105

What are your favorite musicians, bands or albums?.................110

Tell us about your experience starting and running your own business? What advice would you give to people starting their own business? 112

What were you like as a teenager?..128

Did you have a favorite teacher? What made them great? 136

What was your first boss like?..138

Who is the wisest person you've known? What have you learned from them? 140

Tell us the story of your miraculous birth 141

Where is your secret garden where you live? 145

What was it like to move to Dubai from India? How did
that happen and what was life there like? 150

Which people have been the kindest to you in life? 169

What's the first major news story you can remember living
through as a child? 174

Knocking on Heavens Door 176

Would you prefer to have an adventure, or read about one? 185

What are some of your pet peeves? 187

What were your favorite subjects in high school? 188

What are some of your family traditions? 189

What fascinated you as a child? 190

How far back can you trace your family ancestry? 191

Tell us about your travels 194

Do you have any interests? 205

What did you read as a child? 209

What is some of the best advice your mother ever gave you? ... 210

What were your grandparents like?

Starting my story with my grandparents Peter and Mary Furtal who were born in the 19th century. My grandfather was the

direct descendant of a Portuguese settler, Immanuel Furtal, who came to India during the 18th century, and inter married an Indian, my grandfather Peter was a product of their marriage. He had a brother and sister as well. Since I was born in 1949, I have a lot of memories of my grandparents, who were stationed in the south Indian port city of Fort Cochin, in the Ernakulam district. Peter and Mary Furtal had 4 children, of whom my mum Josephine was the eldest. The younger 3 were boys by the name of Joesph, Peter and Clifford. Grandfather Peter was an intelligent, powerful and dominating character, so much so that my nana(grandmother) had no say in any matter, but remained a kind, humble housewife who quietly followed my papa's instructions or orders. Her ancestors also belonged to the Portuguese descendants, called by the name of Coelho, from a wealthy family. Nana was married off to Papa when she was just 13 years old, while papa was 18.

Papa was a capable and intelligent man, who soon rose to the position of director in the TATA industry, where they manufactured different kinds of oils, watches and soaps and more products. My mum often used to take us to papa's place to have a more comfortable weekend with her parents, as we weren't doing financially too well then. Being at my grandparents' place was a good change for us. It was a big house (where we were 8 children, including my parents Josephine and Nelson). After an hour's bus ride from Fort Cochin to Ernakulam, Papa was lucky to witness the wright brother's first airplane that flew into the country at that time. Papa was a very rich landowner, having countless houses and shops to his credit, but he never showed off his wealth and lived humbly. It was in 1959, when I was about 9 years old, papa and nana celebrated their Golden wedding anniversary, when an enclosed family picture was taken (I am seated at the right-hand corner, last line where the kids are seated). Papa and nana along with my mum and dad, mum's brother Peter & Wife, and all of us children in the above and below lines.

As I grew older, I was told that papa was a diabetic and an arthritic patient. Therefore, he was seated on his long easy chair all the time. Nana was healthier, but somehow passed away

before papa in 1964, on the self-predicted day that she was going to pass. She was faithfully religious, and knew the date and time she would be leaving this earth. Hence, my mum was by her side the whole day. Papa lived for a couple more years and then slept in the Lord, when he was about 68 years of age.

The pictures added are 1. of papa and nana when they were newly married teenagers and the family photo taken on our grandparents golden wedding day. All my 8 siblings can be seen in the picture with my mum and dad. My uncle (mum's brother and family is also there) It was a very auspicious day, and indeed a memorable one. In 1987, my mum and dad followed my grandparent's path, and celebrated their golden wedding too.

What is one of your favorite children's stories?

When my sons were young, Andre, 2 and Lloyd 5 years old, we had an exclusive, happy life together in my hometown, Fort

Cochin. When my husband Lionel left for a new beginning in the Gulf, I took up a job at the Naval Kindergarten School for a few years being a school teacher, and would take my children along, who were admitted in the same school. Our closeness increased, since we went to school and came home together, spending all our time together.

Every night the three of us slept together on the same bed. And that was the time I used to tell them a lot of common fairy tales, (which I loved to read when I was young myself), Aesop tales, like Little Red riding Hood, the three little piggies, fox and the grapes, the thirsty crow, the cap man and the monkeys, etc. Besides these fictional stories, I told them a few real-life stories, especially of my very dear nephew who was very close

to me even before my marriage. I loved being with him too. And living in the same street as mine, he would often spend nights with me on my bed between the ages of 2 to 5 years.

During one of those times when he spent the day with me, I encountered a very funny episode with him.

We had a crystal artifact of a fox reaching out to a bunch of grapes (to narrate the story of the fox and the grapes). I told him the story of the fox and the grapes, while he listened to the story very attentively and interestedly. As the story ends, I took the boy back to his home. After he had left, I noticed that the a bunch of grapes from the crystal artifact were broken from the grape vine, and kept near the fox. The crystal glass did not have a fall either. So, the next time Kirk visited my home I asked him if he had meddled with the crystal artifact. He truthfully told me that he broke the bunch of grapes and gave it to the fox since he couldn't manage to pluck it even after so many attempts. It tickled me in the beginning, but later became a bit cross to think of the destruction of the beautiful crystal artifact. And then I realized how concerned and helpful he tried to be to the fox that didn't succeed in getting the grapes.

This real-life story was often repeated to my sons who loved to hear it over and over again, as by now Kirk was a grown-up cousin to my boys, and they loved him for what he was.

My boys often asked me to repeat the story of Jack and the beanstalk. So, each time I narrated it, I added something interesting of my own and got them story books when they were old enough to read.

What was life like growing up in Cochin?

Growing Up in Cochin

A charming seacoast in South India, FORT COCHIN is known for its Dutch, Portuguese and British settlement from the 16th century, of which Vasco da Gama was one of the earliest Portuguese explorers who visited, settled, and even at last, died in Cochin.

It is a quaint little town of about 16 kms in area. There is still a large Dutch cemetery, where the Dutch were exclusively buried, and it is well kept like a museum.

These Europeans intermarried with the Indians, and that is how we, the Anglo Indians originated. We are descendants from the Portuguese on mum's side (Furtal), and British from Dad's side (Jackson) Hence, we're commonly known as Eurasians, or Anglo Indians, a very small Christian community which later

spread to different parts of the world, where they decided to settle for a better, and more comfortable life.

I was born in Fort Cochin in 1949, and belonged to a large family of 8 children, 4 boys, 4 girls, mum and dad (I'll talk about my miraculous birth in another chapter).

Dad was initially in the army (signals), before I was born. But after the Indian Independence war, which took place in the early 40's, dad got transferred to Cochin, where mum lived with my 2 elder brothers,

We had no bank accounts, so mum and dad spent every pie that dad earned on our food, clothing and shoes (which we got just at Christmas time), and most importantly on education.

We grew up not knowing the luxuries of a gas oven, mixers, grinders, fridge, TV, or a washing machine. I would have been around 10 years old when we first got the electric power supply in our house. Specially financed by my eldest brother Brian, who had temporarily started working then. Till then, we used kerosene lamps for all purposes at night, even for studying. We never knew what it was like to have bright lights, until my brother got us the connection in 1959, and then we felt that the heavens had opened up its bright sparkling lights for us. Most people in our street got their power supply around that time itself.

Mum was a hard working housewife, and knew how to manage and handle all 8 of us. A mother who saw to all our needs in spite of her difficult, financial situations. She hand washed and dried all our clothes, school uniforms, bed linen, etc, with the help of a full-time maid (whose salary was Rs 3 for the month). No doubt all 8 of us made her crazy at times with all our needs. When monsoons came in June, and lasted for nearly 4 months with continuous rains for a week or more at a stretch, it was difficult for mum to dry our uniforms and clothes, so she ironed our wet clothes with an iron box filled with burnt coconut shell embers, as we didn't have an electric iron then.

We had our own kitchen garden, where mum grew a lot of vegetables (that's when I began to take interest in gardening). We also had a few hen coops where each one of us had our own pet hens. When the hens laid, each of us were the owners of our pet's eggs. But mum took care of them and multiplied the hens and ducks. My brother Lamby began to take interest in helping mum with the birds, which he later in life ended up taking as a passionate hobby. On account of the hens and ducks, we had eggs in the morning, eggs in the afternoon, and eggs at supper time. Food was always piping hot from the pot with scrapings and all. Dear Mum! She had heaps to cook at each meal, especially when the boys were growing up. In those days, it was poor food…which now is termed as healthy and organic. Hence, we all stayed healthy for most of our lives.

We drew water from a large, deep well in the compound, for our baths, and washing, where dad helped us. An adjacent large pier was filled with water, and a lot of us had baths together in the pier, mostly splashing. We had fun. Of course, we were only between the ages of 5 and 10 then. I remember this funny incident, when my brother Willo didn't want to step foot into the cold water with us in the pier, and would run away and hide. So, we chased him around the compound, caught him, and dunked him in the pier. This turned out to be a daily ritual during bath time, as we were all brought up like that, bathing in cold water. It was all fun, though. We never had serious fights or anger within us.

Pillows were easy to come for us since my grandfather had a lot of cotton trees. So, mum churned the cotton balls in a big tub, making them soft, and then filled them in cases, making super soft pillows for us. Hence, we had a lot of pillows at home. The pillows gave us a good game. When mum and dad weren't at home, all of us took part in this memorable game of pillow fight. The mess we created, and the after effects of it, but we did it again and again. That called for the belt and the cane.

During the night, mum would bring out this huge mat and roll it out flat to fill the whole length of the hall, where all of us slept together. If any of us were sick, we could sleep with mum on the bed. Since my brother Lamby and I were the delicate, sickly ones of the family, we got to sleep with mum and dad most of the time, and we were given special treatments too. From a very young age, I often got asthma attacks, which troubled my mum and dad very much. And also, there was my dear big sister Dyllis, who often tried carrying me during my attacks, to comfort me (though we're just two years apart). So, this was mostly the reason I got the privilege to sleep with mum during most of my younger years, hence building a close-knit relationship with mum.

When I turned 12 years of age, mum made a special vow for me.... To go on a pilgrimage to the miraculous South Indian church of Our Lady of Vellankani. Mum was a very pious and devoutlady. Dad took me to the church, which was about a 12-hour train ride from our home town. Dad helped me fulfil the vow with prayers in faith, and penance, after which we got back home. Ever since that day I never got asthma attacks till date. That was my 2nd miracle at age 12. There were more in the years that followed.

Mum and dad were my closest friends and we bonded well. I always followed their advice to the T, and took it seriously enough that disobeying my parents in any way was a big sin for me. We were brought up in a very religious, Catholic atmosphere, attending mass every morning at 6 am. Even if it's sunny, rainy or windy, mum took all 8 of us to church every morning even during our summer holidays. After

mass she took us to the beach or a park nearby, to entertain us when the schools were closed for vacations.

Never forgetting our evening prayers every day before supper.

Mum & Dad In Cochin

In a small town like Cochin, we had just two English medium schools. One for the girls, St Mary's Catholic High school, run by Canossian nuns, and the other one St John De Britto (boys school). The girls attended the convent school, while the boys went to Britto School.

It was just about a 15 min walk from home to school. So, all of us took brisk walks to school in the morning, came home for lunch during our one-hour lunch break, and walked back to school. After school we got home without loitering. We did our studies and homework related to the day. We had our tiffin, and then went out to play with friends nearby, had fun playing all kinds of

outdoor games with friends, as all of us lived in individual houses with large compounds. There was no TV, or music to keep us stuck at home. I often joined the boys in their games of marbles, spinning tops, flying kites, etc. I was more of a tomboy, and loved climbing trees, and believe me.... Even coconut trees!

On Sundays after school, all of us friends joined for our weekly gathering at the Cochin beach, where we played a lot of noisy games, flew kites, and exchanged simple news of the week. We had simple innocent fun.

We were very well taught and strictly brought up by children. Mum's voice was the loudest, and seemed to have every right to control us. We went with her decisions in molding us. We were not allowed to join in adult talk, except maybe my eldest brother.

On an occasion, one of dad's officer friends were visiting our home to have some home cooked Anglo-Indian food. Before he came, mum instructed us that an important guest was coming home, and that none of us should be seen in the hall except my brother Brian. The guest came, mum, dad and Brian entertained the chief guest, and dinner was going to be served for him. Then he said 'Mr. Jackson, so you have just this son? Blessings to the three of you.'

Mum wanted to give the guest a surprise, and told him to hold his breath, while she called us one by one by our names

according to age, and we came and stood in a line, the 7 of us.... Shocking the guest immensely, as he never in his wildest dreams suspected that there were 7 well behaved children behind the hall door living in perfect silence, so rightfully obeying mum's instructions. Later when I saw the movie The sound of music, when the Von Trapp family children were introduced to Maria, it brought back memories of how mum called each of us by our name.... Willo, Dyllis, Jackie, Sherry, Lambert, Penny and Rency, to introduce us to the chief guest for the evening. After which we had to get back to our studies in silence. The guest was immensely shocked at the disciplined line of children that stayed in the next room without a whimper, while the dinner was arranged.

Physically I was quite skinny, shapeless, and not pretty at all. I was more of a nerd and took my studies very seriously, scoring well in all subjects. Our second language was Malayalam, the local language, and I made a big effort and interest to do well in this language too, even though our main conversing language was English. Hence never gave mum and dad a reason to punish or shout at me.

When I was in grade 9, we formed an exclusive group in class, just 7 close friends, and we called ourselves the Secret Seven.

Secret Seven On The Cochin Beach

As all that we read during that age was Enid Blyton and comics. So, we had a lot to exchange too. Later when we were in grade eleven, 2 more friends joined in and then we called ourselves the 'Notorious Nine'. Not that we were naughty in Any which way.

We were a studious group, helping each other when needed. We sometimes went to a movie, or to the beach.

Notorious Nine In Grade 11

I had inclinations to go in for doctoring....so I approached mum with my intentions. But since there was a lot of money involved in getting a seat for Doctoring (7 lakhs was BIG money then), mum blankly told me that she couldn't afford that amount with just dad's income, as she had more children to educate.

She advised me to become a teacher which was a cheaper education at that time.

So soon after high school in 1967, I took a gap year to do a little bit of untrained teaching, arranged by mum and dad in a convent quite far from home.

Dyllis and I went together to this place called Bhubaneswar, as we both finished high school together.

After getting to mix with a lot of senior teachers at St Joseph's convent, and living in the hostel as a junior teacher (I was the youngest of the lot) nearing 17 years of age, I was beginning to make a lot of physical as well as mental growth. That was the time I actually grew up! Though I missed mum and dad immensely.

For the assistant teaching, and later on handling the class single handedly, we were given a small salary, of Rs 150, which came as a huge amount to me, as we hardly got any pocket money at home. But even with this amount we sent mum a big share of it.

By now, I was prepared to train to be a teacher. As the pupil teaching year was coming to an end, Dyllis and I applied for a seat in one of the best teachers training colleges in Madras (now known as Chennai), managed by the Irish nuns.

I did quite well in my studies there, obtaining 2 separate graded certificates. One for teaching the bigger high school students, and the other for specially teaching and dealing with the younger group, eligible to teach in any European country.

During our holidays, we visited our home town, Cochin, and spent some memorable days with mum and dad and our younger siblings. On certain holidays, we visited our friend's homes, and got to see a lot of other states of India. By now I was growing up physically, a lot more literally, becoming independent, but still not pretty. I was a very simple girl in my choice of clothes, and never tried to make myself outwardly impressive in any way.

When I got back home as a fully-fledged trained teacher after 3 years, I was around 21 years old. Having a 21st birthday celebration at that time was not known, so it passed off as any other ordinary day. By now I was more presentable, and even felt like a grown up. Began to get a few followers (boys), who I didn't consider as serious friendships. Except for one guy who tried to persuade me of his friendship, and often tried to meet me at home and have at least a 5 min chat, no matter how much I tried to avoid him.

After a period of friendly talks, I noticed that he adored me, and wanted to spend more time with me (during those days we were not allowed to go dating anywhere, except maybe to an open beach). Now I too began to like this boy, my first ever boyfriend. A tall, handsome boy, doing his college at that time. But due to his family background, my elder brothers didn't encourage that friendship, and sadly we had to break up. I always took the advice of my parents and elder brothers, as I considered it to be right and just.

In course of time, mum and dad temporarily shifted to Madras, so we always spent our school holidays with them there. My memories of Cochin are vivid and clear in spite of the years gone and most importantly, since I chose my life partner (husband) from Cochin.

Tell us about your Dad

About My Dad

My dad, Nelson Jackson was born on the 28th of Feb 1912. When he was just 90 days old, his mum passed away, leaving the darling little infant and his older sister without a mother. Not long after, his father Wilfred Jackson, whose father was a direct descendant of a British settler, married again, mostly to care for the two little ones. But life was not comfortable for them from then on. Grandfather's wife Bridgette had 3 children of her own. In course of time, my dad, Nelson and his sister were badly neglected, and they grew up in a very hard way. In his early 20's, he joined the military, as then the European settlers were being asked to leave the country. This took some time, and erupted into a world war around 1939. Before that, when dad was around 24 years, he got this proposal to marry my mum Josephine Furtal in 1935. Dad was tall, fair and handsome, so easily got proposals. After marriage, they lived happily in dad's huge ancestral home in Fort Cochin.

Dad & Mum in Cochin

Meanwhile, dad got posted as a signal officer, in Madras. And visited mum in Cochin whenever possible. They got all the benefits and rations that war veterans were privileged with.

After five years, in 1940, my eldest brother Brian was born. And after another 5 years, the 2nd son Wilfred was born, losing a precious son in between Brian and Wilfred. After that the babies came one by one, since the war had ended and dad was posted back in cochin. Then dad took up a civilian job in the Naval Base at the Willingdon Island, Cochin. He travelled in a small rowing ferry, along with a few others up and down the shore for work. Life was not easy

for all 8 of us to manage on just dad's salary, as mum was a full-time house wife taking care of all our needs and never went out to work.

Dad was a perfect gentleman in every way of the word. A very kind father, who never raised his voice or tried to punish us in any way. A gem of a man who never even hurt a fly intentionally. On and off when he was free, he took up our studies, and gave mum a helping hand with us children, as mum surely had a lot to do for all 8 of us. We never had the luxuries of a gas stove, nor grinder, TV, washing machine, etc. So, before the heavy continuous monsoons began (which lasted at least for 4 months), mum and dad cut and heaped fire wood in the shed to be used for the cooking on the ovens during the rains.

Dad was a mild, and loving father. One of his greatest interests was to go fishing in the back waters, or by the jetty where the fishing boats came in. Most often he brought home a good catch that he caught while returning from work in his little ferry boat. It used to be heart rending to see him go for work at nights during the heavy rains and storms. He didn't earn much, but mum managed to feed, clothe and educate all of us to stand on our own feet. We ate and lived a healthy and happy life. Dad loved his daughters very much.

Dad, Dyllis and Myself

He was my best friend, and we got on very well. Dad loved to get his hair trimmed by either Dyllis or me. One day while I was in Cochin with my little boys, and my parents had shifted to Bangalore, I got a surprise seeing dad at my doorstep. It also happened to be Christmas day! I was overjoyed to see dad, and asked him what made him travel (by plane) on Christmas day? He gave me two reasons 1. He wanted to be with me on Christmas day. 2. Because he wanted a haircut from me (I used to give him haircuts on and off). It just explains our closeness and loving relationship with each other.

He was a top dresser. Always with a full sleeved shirt and a hat on. He had a couple of friends with whom he often played card games.

Dad was healthy, slim and a small eater. Always trim and proper. Once a local Malayalam movie was being shot in Fort Cochin town while dad was on his rounds with his friends. Seeing

His personality and being dressed properly, the producer /director of the movie asked dad if he was interested to take a small part in the movie. Dad felt privileged, but told them frankly that he couldn't speak the language. They wanted him so badly, and told him that his speaking would be dubbed, he just needed to speak in English and show the gestures. And so, it was. The movie was produced with all super actors and became a hit. We watched it, and felt so proud of our father. Later we purchased a VCR of the movie to watch dad on it and bring back live memories.

Dad cried bitterly on the day of my wedding, and even on the next day when mum and dad handed me over to my husband, Lionel. He felt that I was going to be separated from him, as I was leaving Cochin and going away to another state with Lionel. But I assured him that we would always meet either in Cochin or Vizag, where I was going to settle down.

Dad Accompanying Me To Church On My Wedding Day - Votive Shrine Of The Immaculate Heart of Mary, Kilpauk, Chennai – 08 June 1974

Dad and Mom Preparing Me For The Wedding – 08 June 1974

It was the 19th of May 1987 when all of us children joined in Dubai and celebrated our parents' Golden Jubilee.

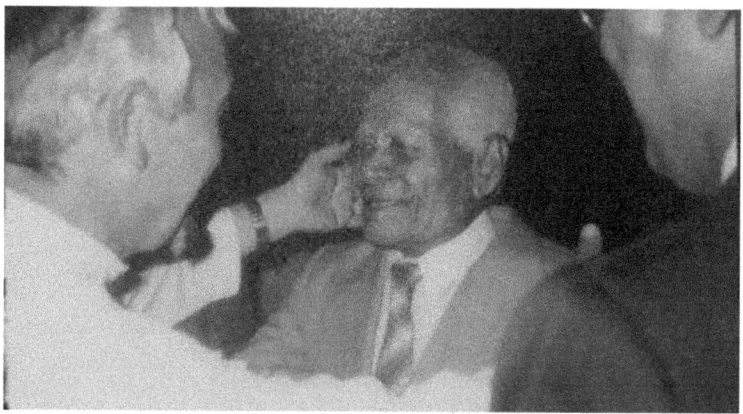

Dad's Golden Jubilee Day With Father Eugene

Dad & Mum Renewing Their Vows On Their Golden Wedding Day- 19 May 198

It was a grand occasion for us children to have our mum and dad with us in a foreign country, to celebrate the function along with our children and friends.

Dancing With Dad On His Golden Wedding

Soon after this grand celebration, dad got sick and was hospitalized in Dubai for a few days.

Dad's Favorite Spot In My Dubai House

He had breathing problems. But it soon came out of it.

After a couple of weeks, mum and dad returned to Bangalore, where they were now residing. In Bangalore, dad was on and off getting asthma attacks and was again hospitalized. On the 16th of Feb 1989, just a few days short of his 78th birthday, my darling dad passed away in his sleep. May his soul rest peacefully.

Tell us about your Mum

About My Mum - An Angel Among us

My mum was the pivot of our family, around whom all 8 of us children and partially dad too rotated. She was our mentor, our doctor, our advisor, our cook, our manager, our gardener, our dishwasher, our tailor, our carer, our teacher, our commander, a philanthropist, and more than anything, our MOTHER.

It was on 25th February 1915, when baby Josephine was born to Anglo-Indian parents Peter and Mary Furtal in the Ernakulam district of Kerala. As a Foreman at Tata oil and soap Industries, Peter Furtal was extremely well off financially. Josephine, lovingly known to everyone as Jossy, was the eldest of twelve children. Unfortunately, only three of her siblings survived beyond marriageable age. They were her beloved brothers, Joseph, Peter and Clifford Furtal.

Right from a young age, Jossy was destined to interact with great, historical and saintly personalities. At age 12 she once had a visitor who came to live in one of her father's houses. Annakutty, who came for a health treatment in Ernakulam. During her treatment, Annakutty was recommended to sleep on a choir bed for reasons best known to the doctor treating her. Jossy became great friends with Annakutty, even as the latter became a nun, and would spend hours with her after school every day, and gladly gave her choir bed to Annakutty. Decades later, Annakutty who chose the name Sr. Alphonsa, would go on to be canonized a saint.

Mum was a blessed lady who lived with 2 saintly people. Her other friend was Mother Theresa who was her visiting neighbour at her Bangalore house years later.

Mum had a forethought that both of them would one day be canonized as saints, and so it came to be. Sr. Alphonsa was canonized in 2008 when mum was 93 years old. And that was the time she told us life stories of her days spent with Sr Alphonsa while she was young. Her joy was boundless to be told of Alphonsa's canonization. In the same way, Mother Theresa was also canonized a saint in Sept 2016. By then mum had already passed away.

Mum's interaction with great personalities was endless, as she accidently got these opportunities. While schooling at St Theresa's, Ernakulam, one of her good friends in class 8 was princess Rajalakshmi, the daughter of the then Maharaja of Travancore. Years later, on a train bound for Madras in 1943, Jossy enjoyed the rare distinction of travelling with Ms. Kasturba, the wife of our freedom fighter Mohan Das Gandhi. Kasturba herself was an Indian political activist.

Kasturba Gandhi

Even before completing her high school, Jossy was married off to my dad Nelson Jackson on 19th May 1937, and went to live and start their home in Fort Cochin where dad had a large ancestral property.

Initially dad was in the military, as it was around that time the Indian Independence revolution was taking place. The country was ruled by the British and the Europeans, from the early 18th century. India now realized that they wanted their country to be ruled by themselves without any foreign control. That's how the

2nd world war (WW2) took place. After the war was over, and India gained her independence in 1947, jobs were hard to find. So dad got recruited in the Naval Base as a civilian.

Dad was the sole breadwinner of our family, until he retired from the Cochin Naval Base. After which my two elder brothers took up the responsibilities of continuing to educate the younger siblings. Mum, our manager knew how to manage the family with dad's small earnings, and stretch the month, until the next salary came in. She provided us with poor, but healthy food during each meal. All cooked and served by herself. Hence all of us stayed healthy.

I grew up watching my mother handle any obstacle life threw at her with ease and elegance. I'm sure she cried herself to sleep many nights, but she still got up every morning and did an amazing job raising us. I could never be weak. After all, I learned from the best.

All 8 of us obeyed her 'Commands', and never tried to walk on the wrong path with her. If any one of us took a wrong turn, he/she was reprimanded. Hence all of us grew up good and healthy, following and living in her instructions. In between all this, mum was a loving, caring and unselfish mother. Nurturing 8 children wasn't easy, especially since there was no money flowing in for a very comfortable life. So, she had lots to do for all of us with little earnings and no savings.

After my 2 elder brothers became working members, life looked more comfortable for us, as they contributed generously towards the family expenses. As we grew older, mum was more concerned about giving us all a proper education, than investing in a bigger house, or having luxurious household items.

Most importantly, mum brought us up in a strict Catholic environment. Taking us all to church every morning at 6 am,

whether it was a school day or a holiday. Rain, or sun or wind, we went with her. We grew up in that atmosphere, so much that most of us attended daily mass, never forgetting our prayers, which we see had a great impact and blessings on all of us.

In course of time as the elder children began to leave the house either for studies, in marriage, or job related, or following their future paths, the house got less noisy and more vacant with occupants. Hence mum now spread her arms towards charity…though she was still a hard working housewife. When my 2nd brother Wilfred left to work abroad, and started sending mum unlimited money, mum felt she could do some good with the extra income, as by now it was also time for dad to retire and settle down.

In a period of 8 years, mum began to adopt 5 boys ranging from the age of 5 to 12 years.

These boys belonged to different poor families, religion, and backgrounds. She began to treat them as her own sons. These boys came in one by one, taking our empty spots in the house. They grew as sole companions and helped mum and dad. While we were children, we treated them as our younger brothers. They helped our parents in the house work, purchasing, and mostly companionship. As they were completing 18 years of age, mum trained them for their future paths. She got one of them recruited in the army in North India, where he was trained to become a soldier in the most dangerous war zone, Siachen Glacier, highest battlefield in the world, facing Pakistan. He used to visit mum and dad during his allotted breaks. Mum sent 3 of the others to work in my brother's company abroad, Dubai. While one of them preferred to marry and settle down in Cochin. Her charitable acts to the needy were boundless. She never wanted to accumulate wealth for herself, as she was very sure her children would care for her, when and if dad passed before her.

In course of time, mum and dad got all 8 of us married to spouses of our own Anglo Indian community, with none of us going against their wishes in choosing our partners in life. All 8 of us settled in different places to begin with, and with mum's constant prayers, all 8 of us were blessed with healthy, normal children of our own. Mum made sure to help each of her daughters during their time of delivery, travelling by herself from one daughter to another at their time of need, wherever they may be stationed.

(Mum attended my second son – Andre's Delivery In VIZAG)

Besides being a grandmother to my eldest son, I also chose mum to be his Godmother, as that's how close mum and I were. Hence this built a very close bond between mum and my son Lloyd

In May 1987, we 8 children had the greatest blessing of celebrating our parents 50 years of married life (their Golden wedding), along with our families and friends in Dubai, where most of us were settled by now.

In spite of all their ups and downs, mum and dad lived healthy and happy enough to celebrate 50 years of togetherness. By now they were both in their 70's, and stayed in perfect health.

In 1989, dad sadly passed away peacefully at the age of 78 in Bangalore. May daddy rest in peace!

Mum was alone now in Bangalore (with all the 8 children having flown out of her nest), she had only the maids and a nurse to take care of her. Hence all of us took turns to visit her every month from wherever we were stationed. It was now time to celebrate mum's 80th birthday.

So all 8 of us joined in Bangalore and gave mum a memorable 80th birthday in her Bangalore house.

After some years, we decided to bring mum to Dubai on visits every 3 months. Age was catching up with her, and travelling every three months was not easy, since she was now wheelchair bound due to advanced arthritis on both her knees. So, in 2005, we had a better idea, and since all of us were doing so well financially, we sponsored her on a resident visa, which was renewed every year. From then on, mum had a relaxed stay with my brother Lambert, who had a better, and more open, spacious and comfortable accommodation for mum, with 4 maids to help her in all her needs, and with love and concerns from all of us children, along with a few of her adopted sons.

Her chief carer/nurse was Gracey, who took care of mum most of the time during the day.

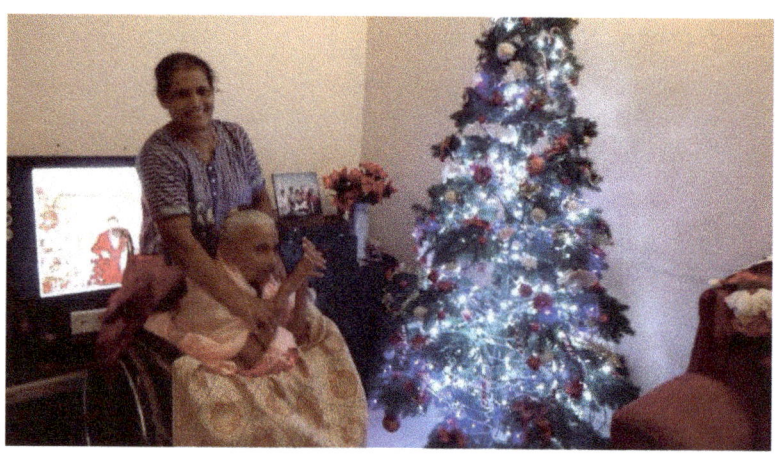

(Mum's Last Christmas With Me and Gracey)

Mum's 90th birthday was celebrated with such pomp and show in 2005, in Lambert's premises, along with our families and friends. From then on, every year we looked forward to the 25th of Feb to celebrate mum's birthday. Her memory and speech was perfect, with no medication whatsoever. Her 95th birthday was another grand occasion for all of us to join in.

By now mum had the blessings to see all her 8 children, their spouses, 18 grandchildren, and 15 great grandchildren.

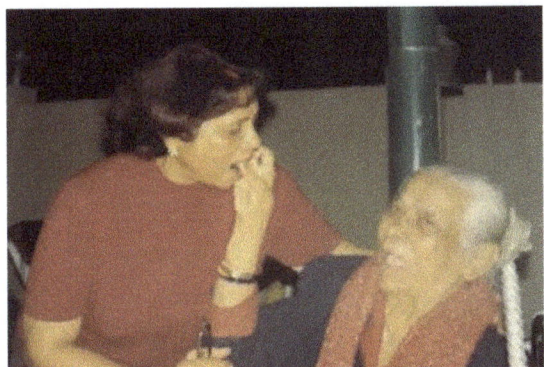

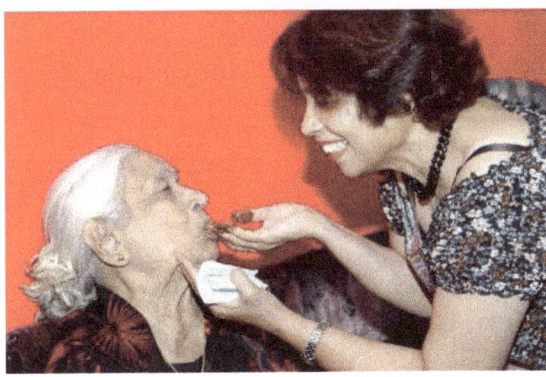

(Mum giving me cake on her 95th B'day) (Me Feeding her cake on my 60th B'day)

Soon after her 96th birthday, we noticed signs of Alzheimer setting in. Age was catching up too. When mum was 98, Lambert and his family were deciding on shifting to Canada for settlement, though he was still busy with his shipping company in Dubai, and with my elder brother passing away, things were getting a bit difficult for Lambert. So, I volunteered to take over mum's responsibilities by the beginning of 2013. By then I had closed my school and decided to shift to India for good, and to have mum with me for as long as God wanted it. Mum's greatest desire was to live and enjoy 100 years of life. God did answer this prayer of hers.

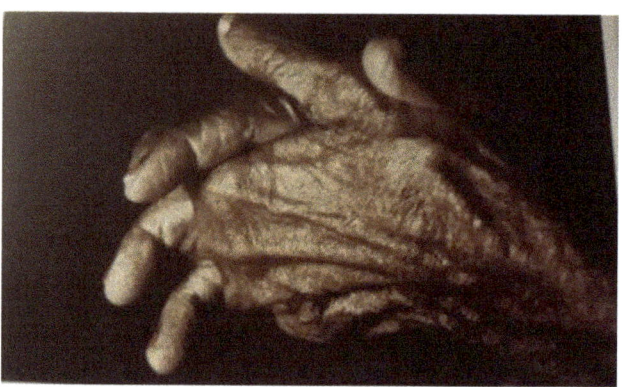

(Hands Of An Angel On Her 99th Birthday)

On 25th Feb 2014, Lambert, me and our families including our spouses and children, along with few relatives and friends around, celebrated mum's 99th birthday with a mass officiated in Lamby's house, followed by a small reception. Mum now commenced her journey to her 100th year.

While with me, mum and I began to bond more physically. I prepared and fed her the morning meal every day. They were satisfying and joyful moments for me, as I now got the opportunity to care for her during her last days, while my 3 children had flown out of my nest.

During my younger days I was a weakling, and mum gave me special love and attention in order to get me on track with my health. Now I had all the chance to give at least a part of what she did for me. As I had her all to myself. There were maids who took care of all her physical and hygienic needs. As the days went by, Mum couldn't communicate at all. We just sat holding and kissing each other's hands all the time. I noticed she was deteriorating as the days went by.

On April 12th 2014, as usual I tried to feed mum something for breakfast, but she refused to have anything. I had this premonition that it was going to be her last day with me.

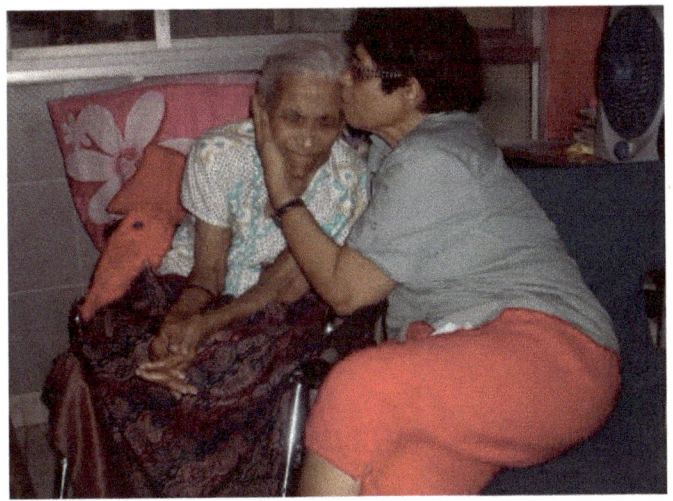

(Mum's Last Day With Me)

Meanwhile, Lambert and his wife Deanne had reached my home too. Around 4 pm, the same day, my darling mum passed away in my presence. She was on her path to her desired 100th year.

I felt so privileged to have had mum with me during the last 14 months of her life. May MAMA's soul REST IN PEACE.

In loving memory of
Josephine Marie Jackson

26.02.1915 - 12.04.2014

*Mum played a different role
in all our lives. A wife, a mother,
a sister, aunt, cousin,
grand mother,
a great grand mother & friend*

*No matter what, the love
we have for her is one.*

*She brought us comfort when
we had pain, lived her life
to the full without complain.
The strength and love of our mum
held all of us together,
even more now than ever.*

*She isn't physically here,
but we still feel her near.*

*In every step we take
and every move we make,
what she has given to us
no one can ever take*

R.I.P. MUM

*From
The Bereaved Family Members*

Were your parents strict, or relaxed?

My Parents - strict or relaxed?

From the little I know, specially in the 50's, 60's, and 70's, at least 50% of the Indian parents had good control over their children (canning them when necessary). The same discipline worked out or was practiced in the classroom. Why? I don't know. But I know one thing for sure —- children with strict parents had a better and more disciplined upbringing; compared to the children of the present generation. Besides, when you're not given into your whims and fancies, you work hard for it by walking on the right path. Parents/spouses' relationships with each other also play a very important role in their children's behavioural patterns.

My mum was very strict with her offspring – especially the daughters. As, during our teenage-adult lives, a woman having a baby out of wedlock was the most disgraceful and shameful act, and talked about by society. That's not the case with the present generation, when teenagers have total freedom to do what and how they want to live, even by leaving their family home and pairing up with their partners. Having a baby out of wedlock is very common now, and even accepted by society. But mum was very strict with her girls, and not so much with the boys. Dad was a gentleman of peace, love and calm —-whatever came his way. So, he never really cared for his children like the way mum did. Mum also got the support from my 2 elder brothers to be strict with the girls. But frankly speaking I did not experience any kind of strictness or punishments, as I didn't give them any reasons for it. We were generally told to have our head on our shoulders and in our books. Hence, I thought it was only right to follow my parents' advice, and therefore followed it to the T.

My eldest sister, who was the prettiest of us girls, got into a lot of distractions (mostly boys) during her school days, which in return affected her studies. Hence mum had to put her foot down, and be strict with her. In the same way, my sister younger to me, also was doing badly in studies, for reasons known to her. She was also on the stubborn side, answering back to mum, and speaking disrespectfully most of the time, and seemed quite unsettled in her behaviour even with her siblings. So, she was known as the 'Black sheep' of the family. If it was in the present times, that particular child would have been given counselling. But during our times, parents had no other option but to belt or cane the troublesome ones.

As a parent myself, and a school teacher as well, I feel there should be a certain amount of strictness and control over our children. As a result of our parents' strictness, (mostly mum and the elder brothers) all 8 of us grew up to be absolutely well behaved adults, without any addictions or babies out of wedlock.

Most children also grow up to be decent adults without strict parents. Recently, I readon international news about 2 sons (in individual categories), shooting their parents. Children are addicted to drugs, substance abuse, drinks and the like, which is easily available now, while we never had access to the likes of this during the 50's and 60's. Besides, in the present generation, the children are aware of the Helpline for domestic abuse in case parents tend to be strict or even try to correct them in any way, and they take advantage. Hence at least 25% of the children grow up doing what they want and how they want it. Spoiled kids can turn out to be masters in crime, or vice versa depending on the individual.Dad was a relaxed kind of a man because he had fewer responsibilities. Taking up the care and concern of the house, mum felt she was more responsible for the children in every way.

She wanted us to grow up as honest, responsible citizens in our years ahead. When mum opened her mouth to correct us, we had to shut ours. Or else he/she faced the consequences. In fact, she had control over each one of her children till the age of 90, during the time when she was conscious of her children's ups and downs in life. She kept herself occupied praying wholeheartedly for each of us in the family.

As a parent myself, my advice to young parents is: not to give into your child fully. Be kind and understanding, at the same time making them understand that you are the parent, and he/she is the child. Do the talking when they need to be told. That way you pave a smooth road for them.... understanding their needs.

How did you meet your spouse?

How did I meet my spouse?

This is sort of a complicated story — —- and I don't know where to start. It was a kind of destined path that got me to link with my spouse- to- be. It was not love at first sight, or love is blind kind of thing.

I was now beginning to 'grow' physically and getting a little deviation in my mind to interests besides studies, as I had by now successfully completed my teacher's training course, and maybe around 21 or 22 years old. Mum used to advise us 'as long as you're studying, have your head in your studies, and on your shoulders', to which I followed her fully.

After studies, and coming home for holidays, I suddenly began to get a lot of admirers (boys). So I began to take interest in dressing up a little (still no makeup or sharpening or eyebrows, etc). Mum tailored our clothes and I was satisfied and happy with them

My admirers were 5 of them at one time, but I never really took them seriously. According to mum, I could chat with them for 5 or 10 mins at home. We had no phones to make calls, no places to go either. I can term it as 'puppy love', or just a crush which the boys had for me.

Finally, there was this tall, handsome college boy, one among the 5 that I began to take a liking to. His name was John, and he was nicknamed as 'John Kennedy' of Fort Cochin, since the resemblance was there. He was mild, kind and loving, and every morning visited me for 5 minutes on his way to college. He was the only boy who kissed me mildly at home, other than my spouse. But due to the family backgrounds of this boy, mum and my 'big brothers' did not encourage this friendship. While all this drama was going on with the 5 boys and my interest in John too, there was this one serious guy watching the whole show from afar. Because he wanted me, and he wanted me, and he wanted me— — but I didn't want him. He was a friend of my brothers, and in fact, a fan of my brothers too, because he was a well-known sportsman of Cochin, belonging to a respectable Anglo Indian family, and financially better than us, which only made my brothers want to say yes if I was interested. But I wasn't.

The boy I really liked even approached mum for my hand, but my brothers didn't want me to continue my friendship with him, for no reasons at all. We just had no choice when it came to our parents and brother's decisions. So sadly, we had to part ways. Knowing this, the path got clear for the 'serious guy' to make his move, such as wishing me as a gentleman would, etc. But I still didn't show any inclination of friendship, or interest in him.

It was the 4th of Jan 1970, when all of us family and relatives were packed like sardines in a big bus going to Quilon for my eldest brother Brian's wedding. Among all my admirers and crushes, my family invited only the 'serious guy'(well, let us call him Lionel now), for the wedding.

The wedding took place in the church, once the reception was over , the family now got ready to leave back for our home town in Fort Cochin. All of the wedding crowd was packed into the bus once again for our journey, except the bride and groom who stayed back at her place. I was the last to get into the bus, and everyone decided that I would sit next to Lionel, which of course was not to my desire. But as fate would have it, there was only one seat left in the bus next to Lionel. I had no other choice, but to sit there next to him. By now he was half way through heaven's gate, 'cos that was what he wanted. It was an eight hour journey back at midnight. After about an hour's drive, I began to fall asleep, and started drooping. Lionel willingly and excitingly offered his shoulders to rest my head on. He hardly moved his shoulders, fearing he would wake me. He held on to keep me comfortable when there were jerks and bumps during the journey. Everyone went to sleep in the bus, except Lionel, since he was seeing that I had a comfortable journey by resting on his shoulder. After a long journey, we reached our destination, with me being a changed Jackie as compared to the beginning of our journey. I realized now that this should be the man that I should love. Not for his looks, or wealth, or fame, but for his patience. He waited for me patiently for 5 years, though I had rejected his earlier approaches. Now he has conquered me with his patience.

My parents and brothers didn't object to him, when he came home the next evening, and asked them if he could walk me to the beach on occasional evenings. And so it was, he got the 'permission' with an excited thumbs up. Slowly, it turned into a path of love for us.

The love story continued for 4 years with both of us living in two different places, and keeping our love going with just our 'snail mails'. Since I was now a full-fledged teacher, working at Montfort Boys High School, Yercaud, and Lionel transferred to Vizag from Cochin. We only met maybe twice a year when I came home for my school holidays, and with Lionel joining his family in Cochin for Christmas. We never had any phone numbers to call each other (1970), but instead became veterans in writing letters to each other. He wrote beautiful love letters to me every day and numbered them, so that I could know if I missed any. He was working on the fishery boats that often sailed out to sea for 21 days. So how do I get the letters for those 21 days? He wrote them all in advance, what his heart told him, numbered the letters, and gave it to a friend to post one every day. According to the numbers on them, so I was getting a letter every day even though he was out at sea. The letters were 'sweet nothings', and I was getting addicted to them. If I missed a letter on a day, it was like the druggies not getting their daily shots. To make the letter episode more interesting…. he sent me a gift when he received my 100th letter. This way he encouraged me to write more. Our love blossomed on our letters, and not with physical connection.

Finally, after 4 years of learning to trust each other, by living away from each other, and being true to each other, we decided to get married and live together in Vizag, and work in the same place.

Since mum and dad were now stationed in Madras, we had our wedding at the Votive shrine of the Immaculate heart of Mary, Kilpauk.

The wedding mass was officiated by my uncle priest, Fr Christopher Coelho.

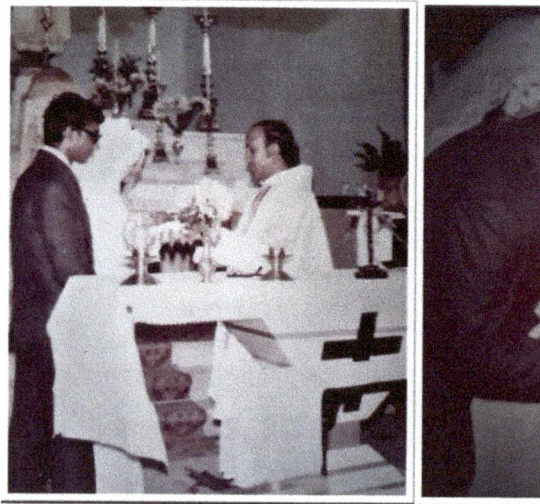

With the reception in a hall the same day, on the 8th of June 1974.

And after a short honeymoon in Ooty, both of us left for Vizag as a couple.

We rented a little house, within walking distance to my work (St Joseph's convent), and happily settled in.

Are you still friends with any of your friends from high school? How have they changed since then?

ARE YOU STILL FRIENDS with people FROM YOUR HIGH SCHOOL?

Yes, as a matter of fact I do/did keep in touch with a few of my high school and college friends. One of them—Jeanne, was my dear best friend from grade 4 right up to high school, and well beyond. After our studies, she settled in Australia, while after a short stay in India, I moved to Dubai. In the beginning, we regularly wrote 'snail mails' until emails and WhatsApp came into being. We visited each other in our citie. Jeanne was a lovely, vibrant, vivacious, positive, and down to earth friend. Coincidentally, both of us chose the same profession as teachers. We were more or less of the same size in clothes, except in height. We were also of the same age, and married boys from our home town, Cochin.

Holidaying in Oz with Jeanne and her husband Victor was real fun. She knew what interested me, so we went to apple orchards, farmers markets, flower gardens, drove through the country, walked in the rain and mud trying to pick apples and plums. Jeanne was a down to earth school friend that I kept in touch with. Our friendship was sincere and concerned.

Then one day 6 years ago, Jeanne called to tell me that she was diagnosed with colon cancer, and had started treatment for it. What could I do? Only pray, pray and pray for her.

Even with chemo and radiation treatments, she continued being a positive and bubbly girl. Always with a smile. I visited her thrice during her cancer times. She had lost weight, and pretended to stay healthy and active. While maybe deep inside, she would have been going through painful spasms. I last visited her 4 years ago on one of my trips to Oz. She told me then that she didn't have much time to go. She usually calls to wish me on my birthday 26th of March. But 3 years ago, she didn't call. So, I tried calling her. The phone was answered by her visiting sister, who told me that Jeanne was not able to talk, and was in her final moments with her family around her. The next day, 27th March as I was leaving for a holiday to Kashmir, I received a message on my phone from her daughter, that my my dear friend had breathed her last. I had no words to express my sadness, and neither could I go. May my dear childhood friend's soul REST IN PEACE.

Jeanne & I in Sydney, Oz

I do have another friend, Ann, who was my college mate. We keep in touch occasionally, as she is also settled in Oz. But never as close as my high school friend.

Ann & I in Oz

And yet I have another very close friend for the past 35 years from Dubai. We were teachers in the same school. A genuine friend who laughs with me when I laugh, and cries with me when I cry. Sadly, now we're far away from each other. She left Dubai for Canada, while I left Dubai for India. But our true friendship stays strong even though we're thousands of miles away from each other. I do visit Canada occasionally and spend a few days with her. Shirley is kind, loving, gentle, and generous simpleton with a clean heart. We do have long talks on the phone. Jeanne, my classmate, was a mutual friend of Shirley and I. So all the more reason that we had this close connection.

And last of all, a real, true and genuine friend in my senior age. Indira. We became close friends when she visited her son here in Bangalore. We went for walks and chatted every day. Coincidentally, she was also a retired teacher like me. Unfortunately, she had to return to her native place. But we keep in touch on WhatsApp and phone calls. A concerned friend I can term as the 'positive elder sister'.

Indira & Myself In Bangalore

I thank God for the wonderful close and true friends I have had, and have in my life. True friends stay forever, beyond words, beyond distance, and beyond time.

I had missed posting these pics for the story of 'my best friends' in my last entry I sent yesterday. Is there any way you can enter these pics, in the para I wrote about my friend Shirley in Canada? Thanks so much. Jackie.

Who are your children?

Who are your children?

God has blessed me with the greatest title ever MOTHERHOOD, three times over, with 3 lovely children…2 boys and a girl. To conclude a perfect family, and I couldn't have asked for more.

My eldest and first born – Lloyd, my heartbeat. The first child always remains special to their parents. Why? Because he gave me this greatest title on earth MOTHER.

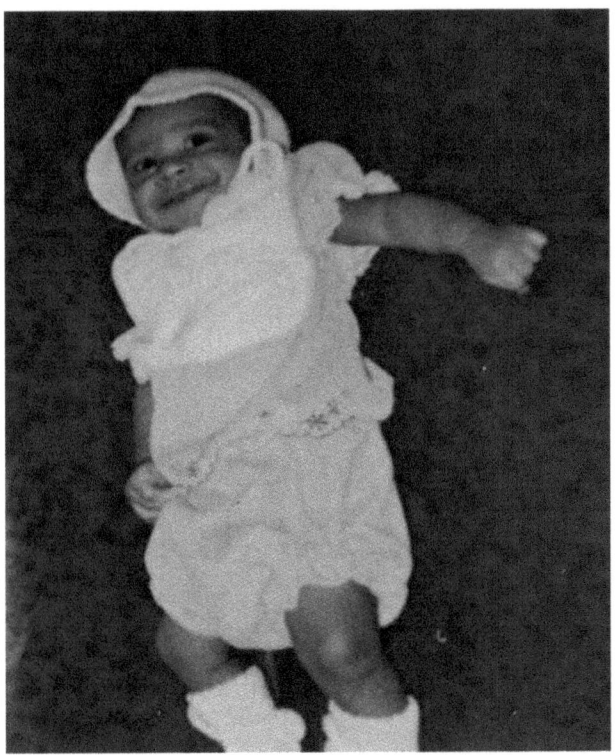

Lloyd was born on the 10th of October 1975, at 8.30pm in a moderately generic clinic in Vizag…assisted by a male gynecologist, with my dear mum watching the whole scene. He arrived much after the due time, and even picked my special date for him 10/10, since it was an induced labour. So, we got him out after 10 months. I guess he was quite comfortable inside, and didn't want to come out, hahaha. A beautiful big- made child! Our first showers of blessings. 10th October was the birthdate of my first teacher, as well as Lloyd's teacher.

Lloyd grew up to be a hyperactive child. Taking part in school concerts from the age of 3, and winning a Binaca smiling contest while at Naval Kindergarten at 4 years.

Lloyd @ Naval Kindergarten with Teacher Cindrella.

4 year old Lloyd @the Binaca smiling contest at Naval Kindergarten.

3 year old Lloyd @the elocution contest at Naval Kindergarten.

He was often getting into all kinds of boyish mischief till the age of 7. The only one among the three who got a little caning from me. But always a loving and caring, darling child. I feel it was the extra discipline that overall turned him into a wonderful child.

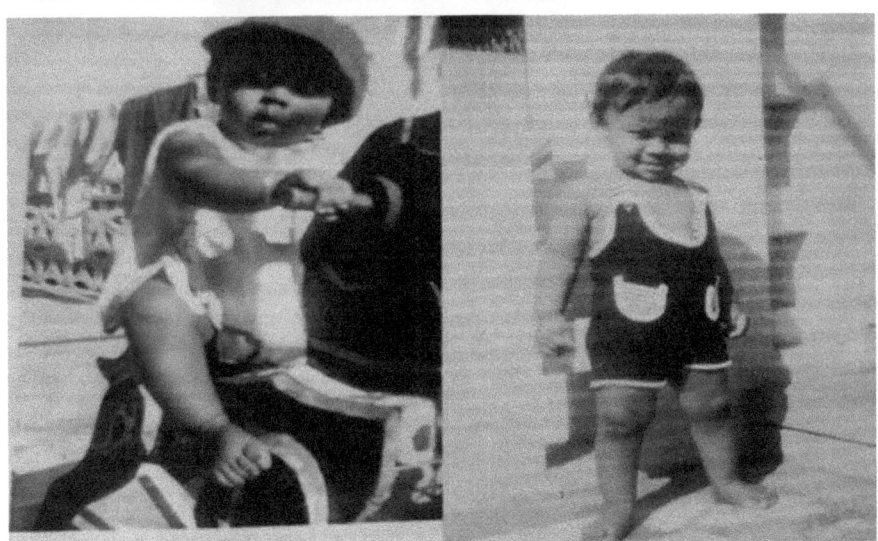

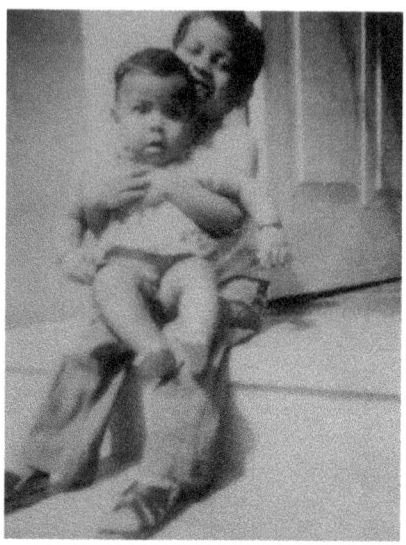

My 2nd born, Andre was born at St. Joseph's nursing Home. A beautiful little hospital near the seaside, on Visakhapatnam coast, managed by the sisters of St. Joseph. On 22nd of April 1978, my water broke while in preparation for labour (PROM), terming it as signs of pre labour, and again went into induced labour for my 2nd baby. So, it was kind of a hurried procedure for his entrance into this world. Our darling little baby son, ever so quiet and just wanting to sleep. Unlike Lloyd, who kept bawling the whole night after his birth, since he was not cozy outside anymore.

Andre at Naval Kindergarten

Lloyd was so well prepared to welcome his little brother with love and warmth, and felt quite possessive of him from his birth. I feel blessed that the same love and warmth is there now that they are in their 40's.

Andre's first year at Naval Kindergarten

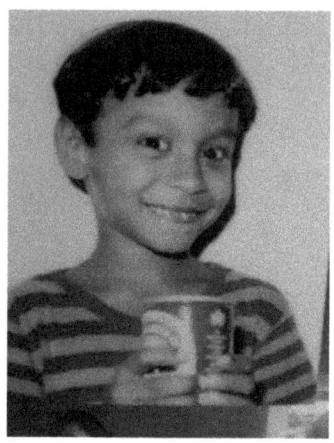

When Lionel, my husband left for the Gulf for a new beginning in a new place, I went down to Cochin with my 2 darling boys, Andre being just a few months old, and Lloyd 3 years old. Three of us grew very close, living along with my mum and dad. It was the best 6 years of our life together.

When they were old enough to attend the nursery, I took them along to The Naval Kindergarten, Cochin, where I was now appointed as a teacher.

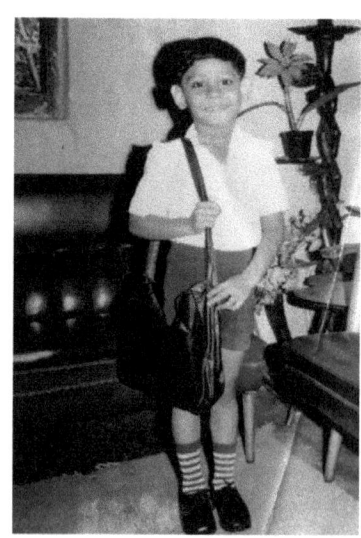

Later for grades 1, 2 and 3, they were admitted in St John's Anglo Indian school, where most of the English speaking boys of Cochin, including their father had studied.

Those years in Cochin were simple, naughty at times, carefree, fun and loving. The bond that the 3 of us created, still lasts. My boys were close knit and loved each other then as well as now. As parents, we feel blessed for that.

When Lloyd was nearing 9 years, and Andre just 6, we left for Dubai to join Lionel, who by now had set up a home for us there to welcome us and continue as a family.

The boys now got into a reputed school, The Modern High School, while I was appointed as a teacher at St Mary's Catholic High school.

When Lloyd was around 14 years I decided to send him to a very well known, reputed, and popular boarding school.... Montfort Anglo Indian High School, Yercaud, South India, (started by the brothers of St Gabriel, Germany), where I was a teacher years before I was married. It was a promise I had made then, that someday, if I had a son, I would admit him in this school.

Andre was still my baby, quite fussy with his food, and needed my care and attention. So, I kept him back in Dubai with us. Though the boys missed each other, and I sure missed Lloyd each time he left Dubai for Yercaud.

By now the boys were well into doing their own things, without depending on me for their personal needs. Also, by giving me a big helping hand in the household chores, like vacuuming, dusting, making their own beds, ironing and folding their clothes, helping me a little in the kitchen, etc. They were, and still are my perfect pair of sons. I miss them so much now, that I am retired, and settled far away from them.

After a gap of 10 years, we got a shock, and blessings to know that I was pregnant with our 3rd child. It sure wasn't easy, as I had advanced 10 years in age. I seriously started working at the school, had started my driving lessons, etc. This time, I was sick for the entirety of 9 months. I was carrying the baby, without a wink of sleep at night, and managing to pass time sitting on a couch throughout the night, in order to get ready for school in the morning, and continuing with my tuitions and daily chores.

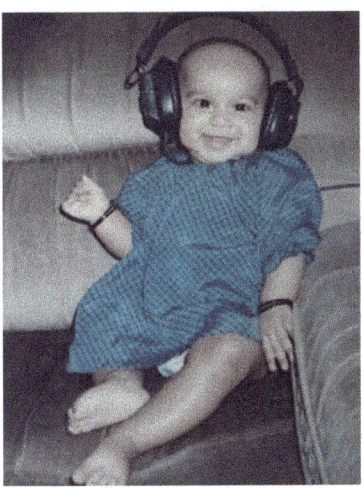

After 9+ months of difficult days, and 20 hrs of painful labour, our pretty little girl, Annaliese entered this world on the 5th of May

1988, 3:30 pm. At Dubai hospital, where Lionel was employed in the engineering dept. We were overjoyed to have a little girl after two boys and a long gap. The boys were thrilled, and adored their little sister. And so did we, her parents.

Children's trophy

Children's Trophy

After a few months of Anna's birth, Lloyd , now nearing 14 years of age, left Dubai to continue and complete his high school at the residential school for boys, Montfort school in Yercaud. He did well in studies, as well as excelled in sports, and extra-curricular activities. Entering for zonal as well as state levels in shot put, javelin, and swimming. Besides excelling in boxing and horse riding. The school had opened up a universe of opportunities for him. Besides, instilling good human and Christian values in the children.

After Lloyd completed his high school in Montfort, he was immediately transferred to Dubai, where he started his Aviation studies at the University of Humberside, Skyline college. He did well, and soon after his graduation, he started working at DNATA travels, which got him into the Dubai international airport, initially as a check in staff.

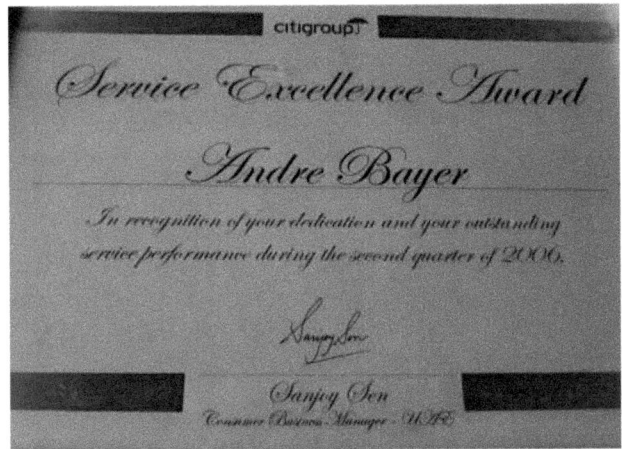

Meanwhile, Andre after finishing his high school, started his graduation course at the international college of commerce. After his first year at college, one of my friends gave him an opening into commerce, by getting him a part time job in the NRI dept of City bank, while he was simultaneously doing his studies at the college. After his studies, he started continuing full time at the City bank, receiving exceptional, expensive awards (gold and silver biscuits) for his performance. We are truly proud of our little son – turned big by now.

By now Anna was big enough to start school, so I admitted her at the New Dubai Nursery to start with. And after a year, I transferred her to my school – St Mary's High school, Dubai, where I started employment as soon as I got into Dubai in 1985. This helped me and Anna to go to school and get back together at the same time.

Anna at New Dubai Nursery

While working at the airport, Lloyd upgraded his status with various courses, like advanced aviation security management from Perth, where he was successfully awarded.

Besides working night and day shifts, Lloyd showed interest and talent in different spheres. He did a successful course in scuba diving, became a semi professional photographer, did movie reviewing, produced and directed short underwater documentary movies, involving his scuba diving sessions, etc. Enlightening us on this are some of his credentials, and achievements given below.

In 2002, he decided to settle down in Marriage at a young age, with the love of his life, Melanie Martins, after a few years of courtship knowing each other well.

With constant upgrades and training, Lloyd performed excellently at work, and obtained the position of Baggage control Manager at the Dubai airport. His rise to the position came as pride and benefit for all of us in the family, which privileged us to travel business class, to any part of the world where Emirates flies, when we wanted to. This way all of us were able to do a lot of travelling, see and enjoy many places, at little cost and in great comfort. Praise and acclamations to our son Lloyd for this blessing. The very first privileged airline ticket from him was a flight to Zurich (Switzerland), my one great desire to visit this place while studying Geography in class 9 and learning about the beautiful, heavenly dreamland called Switzerland. He made this dream come true for me in August 2001. And a lot more umpteen travels followed after this, giving us the opportunity to see the world.

Lloyd's Achievements (and interests) Photography:

Award winning Travel and People photographer with inclusion into the Nikon 100 Most Powerful Portraits in the MENA region. Images exhibited at Gulf Photo Plus in Dubai and Glasgow.

Website: https://lloydbayer.com/ Film Critic:

With accreditation to the Dubai International Film Festival and Hollywood film distributors in the MENA region, Lloyd has published 300+ film reviews in over 10 years as a print and web film journalist.

Website: http://filmphoria.com/ Social media channels:

Instagram:
https://www.instagram.com/lloydbayer_photography/

Facebook: https://www.facebook.com/lloydbayer_photography-110687853650260

YouTube:
https://www.youtube.com/channel/UCphoHfyf1zuEBx6_P11YpxQ

Blu - Maldives Scuba Dive

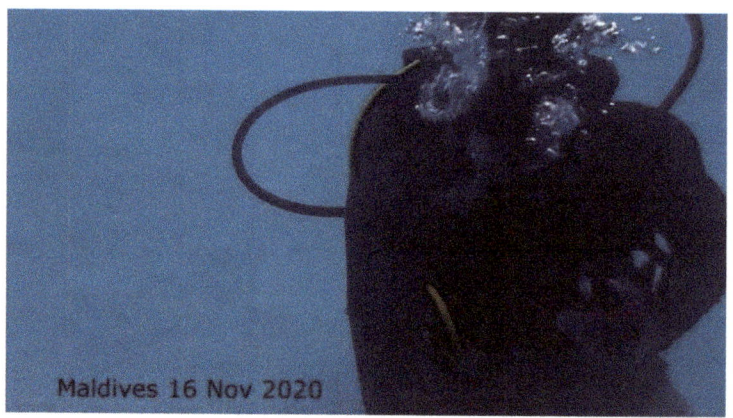

https://www.youtube.com/watch?v=4T3DIM1ryXw No tricks. No VFX. No filters.

Blu is my recreational dive vlog with a bit of social commentary that supports a key finding presented by Leonardo DiCaprio in his 2016 documentary film - Before the Flood. Blu is the work of passion using photography and videography to capture the incomparable ambiance of the underwater kingdom, and to also give these sea creatures a voice.

Hope you find it uplifting 😊 And if you like it, please share so that one day when I'm 80 years old, NatGeo will hire me for one last hurrah…hahaha.

Produced in 1080p and 5.1 surround sound, recommended viewing is with headphones and casting to a smart TV. Enjoy the Show.

Meanwhile, when Anna reached grade 8 in St Mary's, Lionel had turned 60, and got retired from the dept of Health. Since our visas were now cancelled (as we were sponsored by Lionel), Anna, Lionel and I had to return to India. Before leaving Dubai, I managed to get an admission for Anna into Hebron High school, Ootacamund, S. India. The school was run by British, Australian, and Canadian missionaries, and consisted mostly of the staff children. A few Indian business parents, and a few rich folks who could afford to pay a huge fee towards their child's education, were also accepted. Admission into this school was very difficult. But since I was acquainted with the previous principal of the school (while I was once teaching in Ooty), I managed to get a seat for Anna after first being put on a waiting list. They kept to a limited number of 250 children since it was a residential school with a lot of co- curricular activities and studies involved in a British curriculum. Anna made good use of the education given to her, adjusted and adapted well to the Indian environment, the people, language, etc, considering that she was born and grew up in an Arab country. She enjoyed and participated in all the games, indoor and outdoor activities provided there.

After completion of her A levels in the British curriculum in Ooty, we transferred her back to Dubai, sponsored her on my visa (since by now I was managing my own school), and admitted her to a well-established university of Wollongong in Dubai. She did well, and graduated with honors. In her final year, she took up a couple of jobs to earn as well as help her financially to handle her own needs, and continue to fund for her Masters education in Human Resources and business management. We were proud of all her achievements.

She got a job at USEO (united search engine optimization), before working in a couple of other companies previous to this. Soon after, she found her life partner in Aaron Mascarenhas. After a few years of friendship and dating, they settled down in marriage in October 2016.

Meanwhile, after working in City Bank for 10 years, Andre needed a change of scene. So, he successfully opted to work for a local bank—-Abu Dhabi Commercial Bank. (ADCB). He proved to start as a successful employee, and was soon promoted to Credit & Risk Management manager, with a fantastic high salary as well as a good sum of annual bonus for the employees. He takes part in major conferences and meetings with his CEO and superiors. He made us proud, and still does, as he's continuing to be a member of the ADCB group.

Ann and Aaron recently decided to make a wonderful upgrade in their lives, by moving to Canada (from Dubai) for settlement. They got through quite fast andhave already settled in, and even started working. Anna is in a branch company from the same one she was working at Dubai, and Aaron, after a few months of training in project management, has succeeded and started work in a fairly well known company related to more or less what he had been doing in Dubai, called Waste connections of Canada. Hurray for them!

> Dec '10
>
> Dearest Mama,
> Merry Christmas!
> I've bought you this book so that you can start writing your storie like you always wanted to.
> You can carry this book wherever you go and write.
> I love you very much.
>
> Love always,
> Anna

The children were quite aware of my pending desire to write my own story one day. Either before or after my retirement, so some time ago, Anna gifted me a notebook to start writing my Story, which, with the gifted opportunity given to me by Karl, my dear nephew, and my loving, and ever so concerned brother Lambert, I am hoping to put together my past history, holding weight with some pictures, facts and achievements of my children that I have been able to find and produce for my story.

Precious Memories

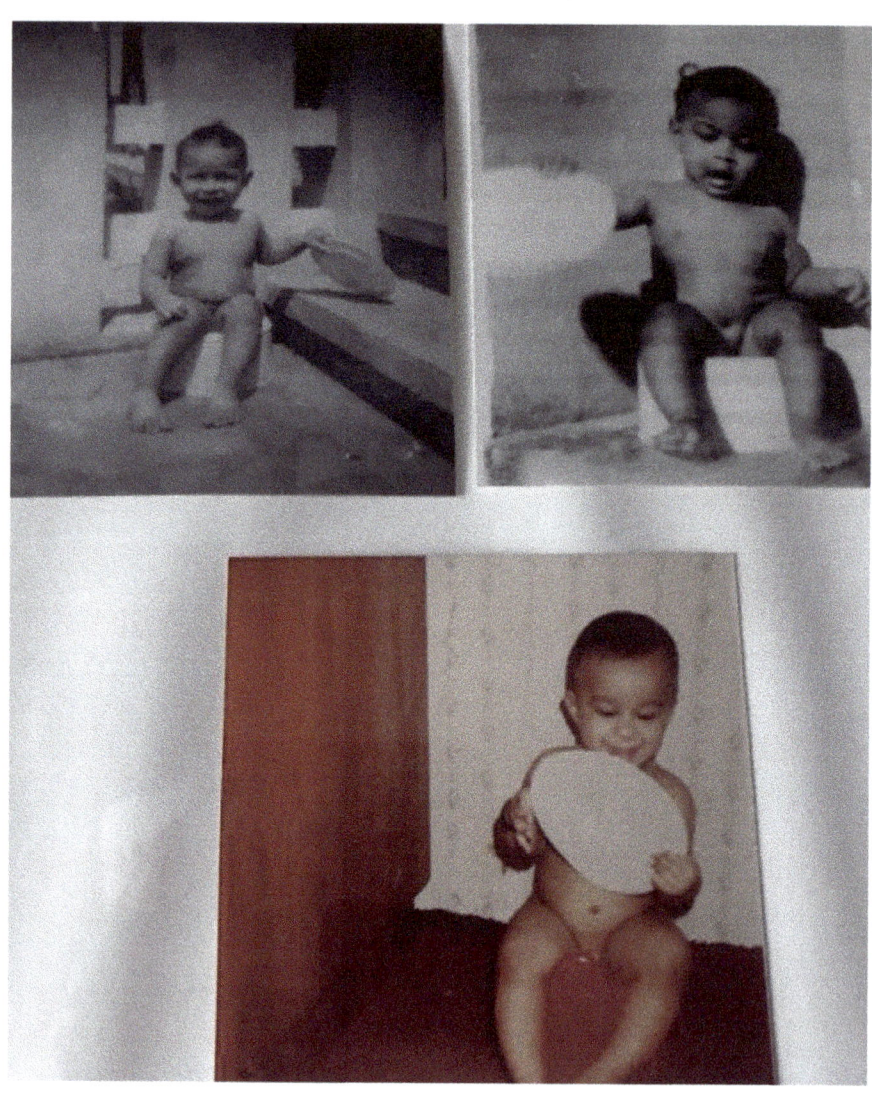

Last family reunion at Prestige Tranquility

With lots of love and hugs to my children Anna, Lloyd and Andre

Tell us about your brothers and sisters

My Brothers And Sisters

Mum and dad did a fine mathematical job of having 4 boys and 4 girls, totally 10 of us crammed up in a 3 bedroom house in Fort Cochin.

Mum with four daughters

Initially, 6 of us older children were born in dad's ancestral home, where we had a very large house, with many bedrooms, a long driveway (with no car), a spacious compound with a lot of coconut trees, and other useful trees and plants. A large well to draw water for our daily needs, until the corporation supplied water to our taps. Six of us older children were born in this large house on home deliveries done by a midwife, as it was in those days. We had a lot of fun times when we were young. Having ducks and hens around. Mum used to get a lot of eggs hatched, and so we had countless baby chicks and ducks permanently. We took turns to shoo away the eagle and kites that sometimes swooped down to carry away a little one. We also had our own vegetable garden. Including a lot of space to run around.

All eight of us

As the family continued growing, and dad was the only earning member, days were turning hard, to provide for our education, food, clothing, medication, and other household expenses.

Hence mum and dad decided to build a smaller house with just 3 bedrooms, and a hall, in a part of the compound, and 6 of us children, mum and dad move in there. While the larger house and the rest of the property was sold for little or nothing. (6000 Rs to be precise)

After moving into our little home, (compared to the previous one), 2 more siblings joined the family. So that makes 8 of us children, and life turned harder – with just dad earning poorly. But come what may, mum provided us with healthy food at each meal, and our education continued.

When Brian our eldest brother, was 19 years old (and still not finished with high school), he decided to stop studies and work, in order to make ends meet for the family's growing needs. Expenses inflated as all of us grew. And one of the most outstanding help he did for the family was obtaining electrical power for our home.

When Wilfred, our 2nd brother (Willo) reached high school, he was just about 15 years old. Brilliant and studious, and quite small at

15. With a difference of nearly 5 years between Brian and Wilfred, mum now insisted that Brian stop work, and go back to school to complete his high school along with Willo. And so it was, with a great effort from Brian, that they finished high school together.

Brian soon took up a job in the fisheries after his high school. While Willo's ambition was to become a Seaman and see the beautiful world where his ships took him. But unfortunately, the Merchant navy did not accept him for 15 years now. Since he was below weight, below height, and below age. The dear boy still had 3 years to grow in order to fulfil his ambition. Instead of waiting to turn 18 for this, one of dad's friends who was in the shipping business sponsored Willo to give him the radio officer's course, which would later help him with Morse code etc. during sea life. Two and a half years later, it made a lot of difference to Willo's development both in his physical and mental structure. He was now accepted for marine and deck training at Vizag port as a trainee seaman. The basic training consisted of scraping and repainting a docked ship, repairing the engines, etc, along with theory and practical studies. That was tough, but with determination and grit; Willo worked hard, and mastered his job in less than 6 months of time. After his course, instead of coming home on a holiday, the company decided to send him to England to start work on the ships there straight away. He was just about 19 years old now, and mum broke down, so did all of us his siblings, as we were all waiting to see our little brother after he left home.

Meanwhile, Dyllis, my elder sister (with an age gap of 2 years), and I, reached high school together at the only Anglo-Indian English speaking school, St Mary's school. She lost 2 years due to ill health and teenage distractions, so I caught up with her, and both of us finished high school together in the same batch. While the boys attended St John De Britto Boys' Anglo Indian school, the only English speaking school for boys then in the 50's and 60's. And is still there till this day.

From the time Dyllis and I finished high school together, both of us became very close, and inseparable. Though I very much wanted to go in for medical studies, mum couldn't afford it. According to mum's advice and instructions, we took a gap year together, in a school in NE India, then trained together, in a teachers' training college (Church Park) in Madras, after which we took up jobs together, at St Joseph's convent, Orissa. After working here for 2 years, and paying up our bond that the convent helped us in our college training, and with Willo's financial assistance too, we left this school and chose to come down south (closer to home), and started teaching in Ooty and Coonoor. This way we stayed close again. Later I joined Montfort school, while Dyllis continued working in Coonoor, as by now she had found her life partner, Lloyd Almeida (since they were both teaching in the same school), and settled down in 1975 Jan in Coonoor.

After about 2 years in Montfort, I too decided to settle down in marriage with my partner in 1974, and moved to Vizag with Lionel, my husband, to make our home there. With a gap of mere 6 months, both Dyllis and I got married in Madras to our partners. Coincidently our first babies were also born together in 1975, with a gap of only a few weeks. I was in Vizag with my first baby son, Lloyd, while Dyllis was in Coonoor with her first baby girl, Wanda.

The younger sister to me is Cheryl, with an age gap of just about 1 1/2 years. For some reason, she and I never got on well from the very start, like Dyllis and I did. She had a lot of behavioural problems when young, which affected her studies. She was stubborn, always unsatisfied, back chattering mum, and quarrelsome. Mum used to punish her badly, and even put her out of the house in the rain, and close the door. But what I admire her most for is that she forgave mum for all that she went through, and loved her as much as we all do. My hats off to her for that!

So soon Lambert caught up with Cheryl at high school (they have an age gap of 14 months). When Cheryl finished her high school, she went in for a secretarial course, but hardly worked, as she soon fell in love with Otto Morris and they settled down in marriage, before her elder ones Dyllis and I were even ready to get married. We let her go ahead. The following year their first son was born. Hence being a total housewife, she never really worked then.

Willo came home from his first trip from the high seas when Dyllis and I were in high school. He had grown tall, sturdy and handsome from when he left home 2 years ago. He came with a lot of beautiful foreign goods for each one of us (we were seeing them for the first time in our life), as well as for the house. It was eye opening to see his generosity and concern for the family. And helped mum become financially freer.

Brian Married Iona in 1970, and had 2 sons in 2 consecutive years, while Cheryl and Otto had their first son in 1974, the year Lionel and I decided to settle down in marriage.

Since Lambert, our 6th member, was considered a weakling in the eyes of mum and dad, they never wanted to part with him after high school, until he grew strong and old enough to be on his own. So, after high school mum got him engaged in a nautical Marine engineering course, which got him prepared for working on the ships in the engineering side. After his course he left for Dubai in 1971, and joined my brother Willo in Dubai, who by now was fully established and enveloped in the marine world. Willo's one great desire when young, was, to someday sail across the seven seas, see the world through his sailings, and finally settle down somewhere with his own marine business company. He was very ambitious, intelligent, hardworking and business minded. So, in 1971 he chose to settle down in Dubai, and stop his sailor roaming, as he saw excellent opportunities to grow in this Gulf state, with the Persian Gulf on the left, and gulf of Oman on the right. Initially, he joined a well-known sea faring company known as Gulf Agency. And after a few years, started his own company 'Ajman Marine services'. It started with a big bang, and did well from the start. Soon Willo invited Lamby to join in as a partner, and between the two of them, they laid an excellent foundation to a legacy. Willo was a man of great sea passion, and made his childhood dreams come true, by establishing his own shipping company along with his brother Lamby. And I am proud to say that at one time they owned about 10 little ships that sailed the seas.

The company fared incredibly well with their combined hard work, and with the help of the workers that were recruited from the Gulf States including people from abroad. For a special occasion the whole family and other relatives were all invited to get together on one of the ships, and we had a gala time on board.

Party on Ajman Marine ship

Next in line was Penny, who came after Lamby, with an age gap of 2 years in between them. She was studious and hardworking by nature. After high school, she went to Madras to pursue her graduation studies at Stella Maris. Since dad was now nearly retiring from the Naval Base, Penny's education was funded by Willo, who by now was quite capable and could afford to help out his siblings with their educational needs. Meanwhile, during one of his long stays in England, Willo did his advanced sea life at Nautical college, Grimsby, England, which enabled him to become a captain on the merchant ships.

Willo married Mayann in 1974. (the same year Lionel and I got married too). Hence Willo's daughter Kookie, Dyllis' daughter Wanda, and my son Lloyd were born the same year in 1975, with just a couple of weeks difference from each other.

Rency, our youngest brother, was still in school and living with mum and dad. While 5 of us elder siblings married, left home, and settled in our respective places, except for Brian and family who continued living with mum and dad in Cochin.

Rency was a keen basketball player, hence had some distractions in his studies, as he was always going to interstate for tournaments.

But still, he managed to finish his high school. After a year or two, he left for Dubai to join Willo and Lamby. Over there, he did a short radio operator's course with assistance from his elder brothers, and was able to start work on the rigs out at sea. He did well, and in 1991, he decided to settle down in Australia with his life partner Jackie Xavier, and later had a son.

After Penny's college education, she too was taken up to Dubai with help from Willo and Lamby around 1976. Over there, she met her future husband in Gordon Almeida, and they settled in marriage in December 1978, and in course of time they were blessed with 2 daughters.

On our wedding day, (8th June 1974) in Madras, Lamby met his life partner in Deanne Fosseberry, and after a few years of courtship, they settled down in a happy marriage in 1979. After which Deanne moved to live in Dubai and joined the Mafia Jackson gang. In course of time, they had 2 sons.

In 1978, Dyllis and family moved to Dubai as well to join the migrated Jackson siblings over there. Intially, she started teaching at Hope Montessori school, which helped her with her two toddler children's education and day-care them too. After a few years, she upgraded herself to take up a job at St Mary's catholic school, Dubai, run by the Comboni sisters.

In 1985, my little boys and I moved to Dubai too to join Lionel, who had gone there 6 years earlier. Initially, I got a job to teach spoken English to the young adult ladies in Sheik Mohammad's

Zabeel palace. It came as a fantastic offer the very next day we arrived in Dubai. Praise the Lord for His blessings, as my life had a 360 degrees turn from India to Dubai in just 24 hours. After one and half months, St Mary's school was reopening after the summer holidays, and before that Dyllis had arranged for a teacher's job for me at St Mary's. So, I preferred switching over to my profession, and started working along with Dyllis. So, once again we were together again. Meanwhile, I had my 3rd child (baby girl) after a gap of 10 years.

After working at St Mary's for 13 to 15 years, Dyllis and I decided to start our own school, with initiatives from Dyllis. We worked extremely hard, in the fiery months of July, August to start. We worked together, and

pumped up life into a fading school Hope Montessori (where Dyllis started work when she first landed in Dubai, and that's how we got the opportunity to buy up that school). Few years later, Dyllis started her own school Bright Morning Nursery. She worked extremely hard, and enthusiastically on her own, from scratch. Her hard work paid well, and after a year, it began to bloom, and was termed as one of the most outstanding nursery's in her area. During this time, Hope Montessori was also performing well to full capacity under my staff and guidance. Those were happy, healthy, hard-working days which also brought in a good income for both of us and our families.

In 1987, most of us were in Dubai, and since it was mum's and dad's 50th wedding anniversary on the 19th of May, we invited mum and dad to Dubai, and had a grand celebration for them at

Ajman Marine hotel, among us siblings, relatives and friends. It was a memorable event for us children, as God had brought us from a cramped up 3 bedroom house in Cochin to this wonderful dream land of Dubai, to have our parents with us on this special occasion in a foreign country.

Mum's and Dad's Golden Wedding

In 1999, Cheryl and family also joined us in Dubai. By then Penny, family, and Rency had left for settlement in Oz. Our weekly gatherings were something we looked forward to in Lamby's house. By now, mum was a resident there, after dad's passing in 1989.

In 2010, Dyllis and family immigrated to Australia, closing up her school. Two years later, I decided to close shop with my school too and get back to India to retire. Mum was now nearing 98 years of age, and Lamby who was all this time seeing to all of mum's care, requirements and needs, financial and physical, along with his wife Dianne, had decided to move to Canada, while his company was still there in Dubai. So to relieve them of all that, they were doing for mum, I volunteered to take care of mum in India as long as she lived (by now she was fully into Alzheimer's). So mum came to stay with me in Bangalore in Feb 2013. She lived with me for 14 months, and I tried to give back at least an atom of what she had done for me. I was happy having her. As all good things come to an end, mum had her last breath on the 12th of April 2014.

Before mum passed, we had this sudden shocking, tragic passing of our dear brother Wilfred at the age of 67, in 2012. The person who brought us from rags to riches and gave us a glorious, sparkling life. Later in 2017, after 5 years, our dear eldest brother Brian went to sleep with the Lord at the age of 78.

From a lovely noisy gang of 8 children, mum and dad, in Cochin, we're just 6 siblings left now. Of which I am the only one left in India now, since Lionel didn't show an interest to immigrate to Australia in 1978 when we were given the opportunity

Though poor, we had a caring, disciplined, and loving upbringing by our wonderful parents Nelson and Josephine Jackson. Mum was a devotedly prayerful lady, who besides accommodating and bringing up 8 children, she also adopted 5 other boys from the age of 5 to 12, seeing to all their needs and preparing them for work abroad and elsewhere.

All of us with our spouses and children

She prayed hard for her 8 children. And one of her constant prayers was that all 8 children get married to their rightful community partners and bear healthy, normal children. God heard her prayers to the full and overflowing, as she saw 19 grandchildren and 12 great grandchildren before she passed away. May mum and dad rest in peace for all the good they did for us children and the strangers around them.

Four sisters

What is one of your fondest childhood memories?

Fondest Childhood Memories

We were all there--- all 8 of us, with mum and dad. Wherever we went, we went together.

My grandfather Peter Furtal once invited the whole family to one of his very large properties in this place called Kalloor, in the Ernakulam district of Kerala, where we were all born (in Fort Cochin). It was supposed to be an outdoor picnic for us. Our ages range from 3 to 18. We were all so excited, and didn't even sleep the previous night, with the excitement of waking up early in the morning and taking a one hour bus ride to this place.

It was like 'the little house on the Prairie', but a little house in a very large area of land filled with coconut, mango, cashew, palms, guava, papaya, banana and lots more trees. Including a large well, and a small half-filled pond.

When the big Jackson gang arrived, it was like letting loose a herd of sheep in a pasture. Mum and dad went into the little house to chat with papa and nana, while all of us ran into the compound. I must've been around 8 or 9 years, and began climbing all kinds of trees, to pick what was on them. (I was a proclaimed 'tree climber'). One of the 5-year-old siblings climbed a guava tree that had a branch sloping down towards the little pond. She slipped down the branch and fell into the pond with a big splash, getting the ole folks rushing out to see the 'tragedy'. But fortunately, there was not much water in the pond, and it sort of cushioned her fall, escaping with just a couple of scratches. There was screaming and laughing and a merry mixed feeling of excitement. It has to be the noisy Jackson family.

Mum cut a green banana bunch, and soon started cooking some vegetable curries to go with rice. Food was not the criteria for us. We felt all the freedom in the world all of a sudden, after our huddled up life in 'Jacksonville', which by now had hardly any space to move.

It was a memorable outdoor picnic we had as a whole family in years! An unforgettable memorable event!

I have a real fond memory of my dad to share.

Dad and I were very close. He was a mild, kind, understanding and soft spoken man. Even though mum was constantly nagging him for some reason or the other, he always kept quiet and accepted his faults.

One of his addictions that dampened all of us was his habit of smoking, even while I was about 7 or 8 years old. He couldn't give it up.

One night, he got into bed smoking,(maybe he had a couple of .drinks too), and dropped off to sleep, without stubbing out his cigarette, which fell on the bed. The soft burning embers soon spread fast. Suddenly, dad felt the heat burning his back, and he jumped out of the bed in a start from his sleep. All of us gathered around him, anxious to see if he was ok. Well, for just a few red scorching marks on his fair body, he was just fine.

The very next day, I decided I was going to do something to not let dad smoke anymore. Young as I was, I wrote a very kind, requesting letter to dad on a sheet of paper, begging him to stop smoking. I sat up waiting for dad to come home after meeting his friends as usual. As he came, he saw me sitting with this letter in my hand. While all the others had gone to sleep. He asked me, "daughter, why are you sitting up so late, waiting for me, when all the others have gone to bed?" I gave him the letter, hugged him, and started crying. He didn't know why I was crying, so immediately he opened the letter and read it. His reaction was unbelievable and heart rending. He hugged me tight, cried along with me, and promised me that he will not touch another cigarette in his life. NEVER SMOKED AGAIN. And we became even closer as a father and daughter – as he realized how precious his life was to me. Dad must've been around 48 years old. We were so close, so much so that he cried bitterly the day I married and had to leave the house to join my husband.

The smoking from young did have its consequences on him. When he was about 58 years old, he started having slight breathing problems, which gradually increased, and he became asthmatic. And later, it affected his lungs, so much that he was on home oxygen inhalations mostly in the night, sitting up with difficulty to sleep. Darling dad passed away at the age of 78, as he was not provided oxygen on time, at the clinic where he was admitted during his last few days before he breathed his last in Bangalore.

Also, I have another fond memory of my childhood, of a friend when I was about 7 years old.

Christopher was the only son of rich parents who lived down our street (in Fernandez Garden). His father was also the president of the Anglo Indian Association of the Cochin branch.

They had a huge compound with a lot of palm, coconut, mango trees and the like, which I loved to climb. (I was a tomboy, and termed as a tree climber till I got married)

Christopher had this huge red toy car that could be peddled with the feet, and 2 seats just for the driver (peddler) and a passenger. There were about 7 to 8 kids joining up every evening to have a ride in this big car. I felt so privileged that he preferred just me in his car every day. He drove around the compound (it was a fairly long drive), while all the rest of the kids ran behind the car wanting a ride too. It is a fond childhood memory because he just accommodated me for the drive. After which he let the other waiting children drive the car on their own in turns, while he went into the house, and I went climbing the trees. When I grew up, I didn't get to see him anymore. We were just playmates when young. Later I was told that being a brilliant guy, he went to college and was the chief engineer on a merchant ship, got married and lived happily.

But sadly about a month ago, I got the information that he passed away. May his soul rest in peace. Christopher was a gentle man with a contagious laugh (I was told so), when young as well as an adult.

How did you get your first job?

My First Job.

How Did You Get Your First Job

When we were young, and part of a large family, with just dad as an earning member, we couldn't pick and choose just anything at all. Be it our career or our partner in life, unless termed affordable or approved by the elders. Since I was a serious and studious individual from a young age, I was extremely ambitious and anxious to become a doctor someday. While finishing my high school, I put this request up to mum. Even my best friend Jeanne came to recommend it to me. Aunty, Jackie is a serious, studious friend of mine, and is highly capable to do her doctorate, as that's her greatest desire and ambition. Please encourage her. But mum told me as well as my friend, that she couldn't afford to send me

for 'Medicine' (which then cost 7 lakhs Rs for the entire course), and also since she had seven other children to educate. Hence advised me to become a school teacher, which would cost her less in terms of financing. So soon after high school, mum and dad recommended Dyllis and me to take a gap year (since both of us finished high school together), and try out teaching in a convent in Orissa (St Joseph's convent Bhubaneswar), located around mid-east India. After which I decide to go in for my teacher's training the following year, or some other course. I had no choice but to agree to mum's proposal. We didn't know where

we were going, and this was the first time we were leaving home, as we never ever had a holiday out of Kerala, except when dad took me on a pilgrimage to Vellankani when I was 12 years, to fulfill a vow.

So Dyllis and I went to Bhubaneshwar (accompanied by dad), St Joseph's convent, on our FIRST JOB. I would've been 16+ in 1967

I was the youngest among the teachers, but somehow slowly began to take a liking to my JOB. If I remember well, my first salary was around 250 Rs. Out of which a part of it was paid for board and lodging in the convent accommodation. A part for our toiletries and stationeries (writing letters and birthday cards to the family members, specially mum and dad), and at least Rs 100 was sent to mum and dad every month, by a money order. We never saved anything, but occasionally bought some material and tailored for a new dress. We made a little extra money on tuition, which if more for the month, we sent it to mum. Once a month or on special occasions, all of us teachers had a treat in a well-known Chinese restaurant, owned by one of the old boys of the school – Jhonny. He gave us a good discount. For my 17th birthday in March, few of my close teacher friends contributed and bought me this gold ring, which then cost just 45 Rs. It was the very first gold gift I got in my life then. The initials WASBD is inscribed on it, which stand for Winnie, Ann, Stella (now passed on), Bernie and Dyllis my dear sister.

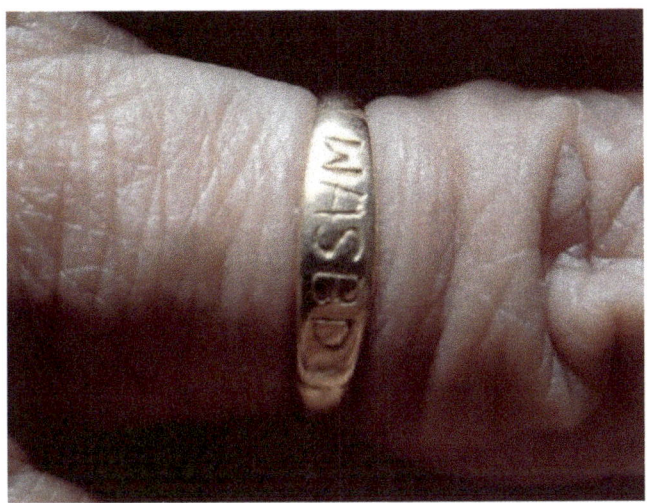

Being exposed from the sheltered enclosures of home for the first time, it took time for me to get used to mixing with the senior teachers, who were already teaching there when Dyllis and I arrived. They used to tease me, addressing me as "baby teacher ". Well, I got used to it, and began acting mature in the course of time. Taking up more and more responsibilities like organizing sport events, parades, concerts, etc. I was getting prepared to go in for my training the following year.

During short school holidays like Dussehra, Diwali, or even Easter, We were invited to our friends homes in East India, since they lived closer to the school province, as we had decided not to travel down south on long journey's (nearly 3 days, as we had a long break in Madras) for short holidays. Hence, this gave us the opportunity to visit places like Jamshedpur, Calcutta, Jabalpur, Chikadharpur, Kharagpur, Kurdha road, Cuttack, and few more.

We were a good group of (mostly) Anglo Indian teachers. We really had fun joking, dancing, and merry making during our weekends, since we were all put up in a large dormitory divided in cubicles (for our privacy), in the convent hostel.

By the end of the year when the term had ended, and the school closed for Christmas holidays, Dyllis and I returned home to

Cochin, to prepare and get ready to leave for our training college in the beginning of the new year.

I do still keep in touch with a couple of them, as few of them are no more.

I also have an interesting few lines to write about my very first earning when I was in class 8.

Malayalam, our 2nd language in school (Kerala's local language), was a must to learn as a subject, in reading and writing. But it was the most difficult language to master, both in writing as well as in pronunciation, and reading. I took it as a challenge, and showed a lot of interest in spending more time in this particular subject compared to the others. I did well, and sure enough mastered it. So mum requested me to help the younger siblings

in reading and writing Malayalam. One of our neighbor children wanted help with the language too. I was most willing to help. So at the end of the month, when this local girl of grade 4 was beginning to improve in the language and get better marks, her mother was so thrilled at her performance that she gave me something as a salary. I was shocked, but accepted it, as I was so excited to receive a "salary" of Rs 3 for the month. I was so thrilled with my 'first salary', and gave the full amount to mum. That's what we used to do when we got a cash gift or won a prize at the sports events we took part in while young.

What are your favorite musicians, bands or albums?

Something little about my favourite singers, Musicians, Bands and Albums Real music was introduced into the Jackson family life in late 60's, when Willo, our shippy brother came home from his first trip back as a fully-fledged sailor boy. He brought home a record player (besides a lot of other gifts for all of us), with a lot of long playing (LP's), as well as single playing records (45 RPM). At that time, some of the high scoring singers were.... Jim Reeves, Cliff Richard, Elvis Presley, Hank Locklin, and few more. They all sang meaningful country, and rock n roll songs, which left nostalgic imprints and memories till this day, for folks of my age group.

Scores of young singers, musicians and bands came in one after the other from the mid 80's, to which I never took much interest.

My husband Lionel is more music oriented. So most often he puts on very interesting, mind soothing country music, which I heartily enjoy.

Some of my favourite singers/musicians are. Jim Reeves, Cliff Richard and the Shadows, Elvis Presley, Hank Locklin, Hank Williams (the very first country singer), and Buck Owens. They were mostly individual singers with musical accompaniment groups. Even though most of these famous, meaningful singers have passed on, their songs and music is still alive among the oldies like myself.

I also do listen to country singers like Alan Jackson, George Strait, Carrie Underwood, Johnny Cash, Merle Haggard, and more.

It was great to see some of these country singers in live performance at the Grand Ole Opry at Nashville Tennessee in 2013 when we visited my most favourite country, the United States of America. We also visited the Country Hall of Fame in the same place.

My 2 favourite bands were (and still is) Bill Black's Combo, and the Ventures.

Tell us about your experience starting and running your own business? What advice would you give to people starting their own business?

My Experience Starting and Running My Own Business

It all started in the sizzling summer month of July on the 1st July 1997, when my sister Dyllis, and I decided to close shop with our teaching at St Mary's Catholic school, Dubai,where we were teachers for about one and half decades), at the end of our school year June 30th, and start on the joys, hope and success of investing in our very own school in Dubai.

Since we were both in it together equally, both physically and financially, and both in the same profession of teaching, we were quite positive that with hard work and cooperation, we would do good in the long run.

There was only one minus point. When we took over a running school from one of Dyllis' friends, the school was functioning in a state of unrelenting bleakness. There were just 9 children and a teacher holding on to the fort of this aged, well known Hope Montessori school that had performed to perfection during its blooming years of the 70's and 80's, owned by an Iranian lady. Sadly, the owner and Principal of the school (who happened to be a good friend of Dyllis), got seriously ill with cancer, for which she had to make frequent trips to the UK. Hence the neglect, and responsible management of the school came down drastically. That's when Ms. Zainab approached Dyllis, enquiring if she could buy up the school. Dyllis was kind enough to share the news with me, and if we could both be joint owners of the school by investing

50% each in our shares of this new venture. Since both of us were truly in the teaching profession, and weren't reaching anywhere with our meagre earnings at St Mary's, I gladly joined in. We shook hands, paid up the requested amount, and became owners of a Business, or better said, became owners of our own school, where we could continue being teachers, and do things the way we wanted it in our chosen profession.

Children learning using Montessori apparatus

We started as summer classes at HOPE MONTESSORI for children of all age groups, who belonged to different schools, (since all schools were now closed for summer in the gripping summer heat of Dubai). There were no other summer classes organized anywhere then, so parents grabbed the opportunity of registering their children for the summer.

Dyllis surrounded with some of the children

Children of different age groups came in by the dozens. We accepted children from the age of 3 to 13 years. Soon class rooms of Hope Montessori were packed. We planned and programmed class rooms as well as outdoor activities for the children according to their age group. We took them to swimming pools, splashes, malls, indoor play pens, etc, and a lot of classroom activities.

The numbers of children were increasing rapidly, so we had to borrow a sister school to accommodate the grown-up children---

as their activities differed. We employed some teachers too, whose schools were closed for summer, and who volunteered to help us run the school smoothly. Some of them were our close friends too. And they were given a salary.

Dyllis and I worked tirelessly in the summer heat that went up to 50+ degrees during these months. July and August are known for unbearable hot days in the UAE (that's why all schools close during these months). But we bore it all, as this was just the beginning of a number of years to follow.

The parents were overjoyed to observe their children kept educationally and actively occupied during these months.

The Jackson sisters were remarkably spoken about because of the enthusiasm and hard work we had put into the summer activities. Finally, by 31st of August the summer classes came to an end, as it was time for the children to return to their various schools for the beginning of their academic year in September.

We started with our regular school on 1st September. What an encouragement! With a lot of new admissions on the very first day.... as a result of the successful and well-organized summer classes.

In the beginning, Dyllis and I worked as Principal/Directress, teacher, nurse, and nanny. Helping each and every child whenever needed. We took in another teacher and divided the children into two classes. We also worked as PRO's and purchasers. Even the labour office and immigration work was done by both of us. We never just sat on our chairs, but were on our feet from morning till evening, as there were a couple of day-care children to be taken care of after class hours. Our combined effort of care and concern for the children was the talk among the parents. Fortunately, we were located in the central area of Bur Dubai--- a busy commercial as well as residential area. It was just walking distance for the parents around the area to bring their children in. By word of mouth, more admissions came in from further places too, so we arranged a school bus for children who were at a distance from the school.

Admissions began to pour in, and we were overjoyed to notice how hard work paid off.

We never once considered ourselves as owners of the school, or left the work to be handled by the employees. But worked equally with them.

As the years passed by, we became the 'talk of the town school/kinder. Admissions came in fast, by the dozens every day. Finally, in course of time, we had in total 23 staff members, including teachers, assistant teachers, nannies, nurses, and a doctor. When we reached the highest capacity of 250 children, we had to close admissions due to lack of space in our little villa school. But the callings for admissions continued every day, so we took down the name and number of the parents, promising to call them back soon. When the number on the waiting list rose to 100 children, I decided to have afternoon classes, starting with assembly and the usual daily program of the morning session. I asked the parents if they were willing to admit their children for the afternoon classes. They were more than overjoyed to bring in their children for the afternoon session. This was because of the education and activities that we conducted along with the staff. A lot of the teachers agreed to continue working for the afternoon classes too, so that they would earn a double salary. I was happy about it all, as it kept me busy in mind and body, though at the time it was quite stressful for me, organizing school activities as well as doing outside legal work too. But my health was good (Praise God), and I managed it alone. By now, Dyllis had opened her own school and was managing it by herself. Being professionally teachers, we knew exactly how to manage the schools. But in a school dealing with young children, we, the management and staff have to be 100% alert, as there COULD BE

ACCIDENTS! Running a school had its ups and downs as in all other businesses.

We started the school program every morning at 8 am with an assembly, where all the children and staff assembled for morning prayers, followed with lots of action songs, rhymes, singing, storytelling (giving children the opportunity to develop their talents), etc, accompanied with piano music played by our music teacher. After which, the children marched class wise to their classes, and then carried on with their classroom activities. Indoor and outdoor activities were planned in advance and given to teachers on excel sheets.

Every year, we conducted three major school functions where parents were invited. The enthusiastic parents were very cooperative with all our school decisions and activities. We had the annual Christmas function, where the Christmas tree was beautifully decorated by all of us.

Each child was given a gift according to his/her age group, and the parents were provided with tea and snacks. Each staff member was given a cash gift, while our most jolly and active Santa (Lloyd Almeida who, most faithfully was our Santa Claus for the season every year) kept the crowds in laughter and merry making, who also was given a special gift.

Sometime around January, we had the fancy dress competition, in which the parents took a very active and enthusiastic part in dressing up their children for the competition. Prizes and certificates were given for the winners.

Our Sports Day was usually conducted in February, on account of the pleasant climate. Children are prepared for this occasion from the month of October/November. It involves each class taking part in different group dancing, singings with colourful costumes. March passed for the whole school accompanied by their teachers. Sports activities with competition games, and picking the prize winners who were awarded with certificates and trophies. All watched by the parents in our huge outdoor premises.

Towards the beginning of March, a grand graduation ceremony was held for the outgoing students. Our proudest moments for the parents, children as well as us staff of the school. It was like an annual day celebration, where children took part in skits, dramas, singing, and dancing. Graduation certificates were presented to each outgoing child. Their proudest moments! And more still, for their parents.

While running a school, parents, children, and staff (giving them incentives and salary increase annually) have to be kept equally happy and satisfied. We, as managers of the school, had plenty to keep us occupied. We had no specified work hours for the smooth running of our business. We had to be dedicated, and prepared to work overtime even in 50 + degrees during the sizzling summers.

Since both Dyllis and I were trained teachers we managed the school professionally. The school timings were from 7.30 am to 1pm, and after a lunch break of half an hour, the afternoons continued into day care, for children whose parents were working late. So, we had nannies and assistant teachers, as well as a full time nurse taking care of these children, seeing to their lunch, toiletry and afternoon rest. After which they had some playtime until their parents picked them. After their work hours, I stayed back most often to manage the situation in school.

My advice to people starting their own business is work hard along with your staff, which encourages them to work actively too. Even though I gained the title of a Principal in my own school, and had an office of my own, I was not always there. When the secretary, administrator was on leave, I took their place. When a teacher was absent, I took her place too. I helped the nannies with the children when needed, and did a lot of our jobs too, as I was a PRO when needed too. It was quite stressful at times. But that's the ups and downs of having your own business. There were no allotted working hours for us as managers. But I can proudly say that at the end of the very first year, we hit a profit after all our expenses.

If we are fully involved in our business, we know where the profit or loss stands. When you start your own business, immerse your whole self into it without just waiting for the profits. It may take years to break even (depending on the type of business). Some businesses are involved in a lot of purchasing of materials or goods (e.g. a green grocery), and the profits fall on the selling of those goods. If they are perishable, then you lose, and go below your cost if the goods are not sold on time. But running a school was different. We didn't have much outgoing expenses besides paying the staff salaries, paying up utility bills, and rent of premises, cost of stationery and other initial expenses. Hence our profits rose to a good graph each year gradually as the

the number of children increased by leaps and bounds. At the end of each educational year, a grand dinner was arranged in a big hotel for the benefit and gratitude towards the hard work of the staff. Once our annual dinner was arranged on a local cruise, we MUST make our staff happy and content in order for them to volunteer and work satisfactorily.

Preparing ourselves to go for the cruise

Finally, after 16 years of handling the school, and since Dyllis was also leaving the UAE, I decided to call it quits too, retire and take care of my aged mum, who, all this time was under my brother Lambert's care. So, I sold the school for a good profit compared to

the investing at the start, and shared it equally with Dyllis. But I must say, I enjoyed being with kids all the time, all my life, as that was the profession I chose.

During an interview with the editor of Gulf News on August 18th 2003

What were you like as a teenager?

What were you like as a Teenager

Most girls count the years and days to pronounce themselves as a teenager, because then they feel they are not a child any more but a semi-adult and feel grown up. For me, I never ever waited to be a teenager, as I didn't know when that was going to be. I was not conscious of anything at all. As a teenager, I was skinny, figure less (wasn't conscious of a figure either), and not pretty or lady-like at all. A contemptible person who lacked social skills, and boringly studious. In other words…. A Nerd!! I wasn't physically grown until I was 16 and in high school. So I was not aware or conscious of a figure, nor was I interested in dressing. So, I joined the boys at play, behaved like a boy, and played all the games they played—like with marbles, tops, kite flying, catching tiny fishes and tadpoles from the gutters along with the boys, and more than anything—-tree climbing (even coconut trees). Hence I was termed as a Tomboy. My mum thought that I was going to turn out to be a boy, and she even took me for a few physical checkups. When I was not playing with the boys, I was with my books most of the time. Mum instructed us that we girls couldn't indulge in boyfriends as in BOYFRIENDS. She meant no physical or social contact. So I obeyed her fully. My boyfriends were just playing games. Since I was not pretty, no boy had any attraction to me till I was 16+ and in high school… and all I read was comics and Enid Blyton. Mum used to tailor my clothes, and I was quite content with her choice of clothes and shoes for me (that we got just annually at Christmas, and nothing for birthdays either). But I did extremely well at school. Not once did mum or dad ask me to sit with my books. At my age, I concluded (according to mum), that's all I had to do, and occasionally help mum with the cooking, that I was keenly interested in. As a result, in later years, I won a grand prize for an international cooking contest, and many other smaller prizes.

From class 8, I used to teach my younger siblings, help them complete their homework and other studies. I was a very fussy eater, hence always stayed slim… or at that time known as 'thin'.

In high school, I was in this gang called 'Notorious Nine'. All the girls were of a much better figure at 16 and 17, except myself.

But all 9 of us were the most studious girls in the class, and that's how all 9 of us joined up and formed the gang. (birds of a feather flock together). We were not notorious in any way. We just wanted another word to go with nine, as we were also termed as the N squared gang. Some of them were quite wealthy, whose parents were business people, and owned cars. So occasionally, all 9 of us crammed into an ambassador car (the most common car in the 60's), along with the driver, and went for a movie, or to the beach, or for a chit chat to one of their houses. Not to mine. I wouldn't dare invite them, as I belonged to a family of 10 members (including mum and dad), and we had no place to entertain any one, (not even to swing a cat), as we were on the Not –to do- well- side.

As soon as I finished high school at 16+, mum packed us (Dyllis and me) to a far off convent, completely different local language, in Orissa (nearly NE India., for a gap year of teaching as well as earning, and then get prepared and old enough to go in for my teacher's training the following year.

Dad took us to this place (Two and half days train journey). St Joseph's convent. I noticed the teachers were all in their 20's, 30's and 40's. I was the youngest of the lot, and still with no figure at all. But getting to mix with these senior teachers, in course of time, brought me out of my shell. At times, they used to tease me to the point of making me cry at times, and at the same time loved me

like a little sister. For my 17th birthday, a few of them chipped together Rs. 5 each and bought me a gold ring, for Rs 45, which still fits my ring finger, with their initials on it. In return, I gave them a little treat at Johnny's Chinese restaurant (which was owned by an ex-student of the convent).

Most regularly we had the same thing on our treats — — Mixed Chinese noodles, which cost about 35 Rs for a dinner for 5. That's all I could afford, after getting a small salary of Rs 250/-, of which we had to pay for our board and lodge at the convent, money order for mum every month, our toiletries, stationery. Occasionally, a Hindi movie, which was Rs 3 a ticket, and once in a blue moon an English movie. That's when I saw Dr. Zhivago.

I noticed, most of the teachers were receiving letters from Pen friends—Nobody had the freedom and permission to have a boyfriend, or meet boys, since we lived in a convent. We had this Junior Statesman weekly, where names of pen friends were published every week. So, I joined the gang of teachers who had pen friends, and I chose a boy (who lived in Calcutta), not very far from where we were located. He was a Bengali called Priyabratha Ghosh. A mature, educated boy, who was still pursuing his studies. A knowledgeable boy, who taught me a lot in Black and White. It was my very first distant relationship. A very modern, educated, and well-read character with a good command of English. Our letter writing increased, and we became addicted to each other's letters. Often the other teachers' friends used to hide his letters, open it and read it out loud during our recreational gatherings in our common room. Being the youngest kid as I was, I had to bear up with all the ragging and teasing, and accepted it in a positive and friendly way.

When we completed a year of pupil teaching at the convent, we went back to Cochin to spend our first vacation with the family for Christmas. Mum noticed a lot of physical and mental development in me, so much she didn't recognize me when I got into the house. After a couple of weeks, it was time to join our training college in January. I was now 18+.

Church Park training College, was being run by the Irish nuns. I was once again going into a convent. We were under strict vigilance, and since most of us were around this age, we had to give it in writing that we only kept correspondence with our parents and siblings with the same surname (Jackson).

The senior girls who were in their early 20's and had boyfriends, had to sever all relationships (correspondence) with them. As we were all in a cloistered convent hostel... having to follow all the rules of the college. As a result, my pen friend relationship too went for a toss, and we never got back to writing anymore.

It was an arduous 4 years of college studies crammed into 2 years of continuous studies, as we had 3 kinds of training to prepare for. 1) The Froebel European education from Kg to grade 3. 2) Middle grade education from grade 1 to grade 8. 3), and the high school education from grade 1 to grade 10. A lot of girls opted only for the middle grade education, because they couldn't cope with the excess studies of all subjects plus teaching related studies in theory and practical. But I took it as a challenge and opted for all 3 courses. All that we did was study and study and study till midnight. 3 days before our exams, we were not allowed to open our books.

Our body and mind had to relax. So during these days, we were taken for a movie, or an European opera (we were usually ushers) or to the British Council for browsing through knowledgeable books. I also remember watching Sound of Music while we were in Church Park. It was also during this time we watched live the launching of Apollo 11 in July 1969, at the British Council in Madras.

At the end of the 2nd year, I came out successfully in all my chosen training sessions. While a lot of the girls who attempted had failed. I don't blame them, as it was one of the toughest studies one could have gone through. Besides theory, we had umpteen practicals, teaching lessons, art and craft, making creative objects out of crap and scraps. Preparations for practical exams, teaching lessons in the presence of the inspectress of education, etc.

After my training, and living in the midst of various types of girls from all over India (most of them pretty and figury), I got to change a lot, as I was now 20 + (still no boyfriend). Now I began to get conscious of my sudden growth in mind and body (the 2 years did change me). And sure enough I began to get a lot of admirers, but frankly never choose anyone for a couple of years, Instead kept them hanging on a string like puppets Hahahahahah.

Did you have a favorite teacher? What made them great?

Here with, my favourite teachers Did you have a Favorite Teacher In fact, I had a few favorite teachers--- Miss Celine Thomas, my religion teacher. She was a very mild and kind human being. Every Sunday afternoon, it was mandatory that we attend the Sunday school catechism classes organized by St Mary's school, where I was a student. I made sure to attend it very regularly, even though instructors varied most Sundays, Miss Celine was there regularly.

In 1964, the first Eucharistic Congress was to take place in India for the first time, and Pope Paul the VIth was the chief official coordinator guest at this grand Catholic gathering, that took place in Bombay, where most of the bishops, cardinals, priests and nuns of the country were interested in taking part. It was indeed a golden opportunity to attend this function. Few of the nuns, teachers and senior students were going for this grand, once in a lifetime gathering of religious people. In the whole school at St Mary's, only 1 child was privileged enough to be chosen to attend this function free of charge, on certain conditions. She should have had 100% attendance in the Sunday school classes, and obtained the highest average marks for the whole year in religion classes (which was an important subject in school, since it was a Catholic Convent.) Miss Celine and the school superior came to my house to announce to my mum that I was the privileged one to be chosen as that child. Just one student in the whole school. I was in grade 8 then. Do you think mum would have agreed to send me? A big NO. She told Miss Celine and the superior that I was a sickly girl, and in no way she would send me for 5 days to Bombay, even though the teachers assured and guaranteed her that they would take good care of me. And that I didn't have to make any payments. I was too young then to realize that I had missed a golden opportunity in my life by not attending the Eucharistic Congress Council. Miss Celine was so disappointed!!

Another favorite teacher was Miss Gauri, our Malayalam language teacher. It was the most difficult of all the languages in India, to read as well as write. Though Miss Gauri was a ruthless teacher to most of the girls in class, she had a soft corner for me, because she noticed that I was making a great effort to learn the language. And for her sake, I took it as a challenge to master the language. So much so, I scored well in every test and exam. She took me as an example to the rest of the class, especially the children who communicated in Malayalam in their homes, and still fared badly at reading and writing. I made a great effort to learn to read and write, mostly because of her consideration for me. Since it was our second language, it was mandatory that we passed the subject.

There were a few more kind teachers that I got on well with. Mrs Connie Eustace, Stacey's grandmother was one of those.

What was your first boss like?

Just a few lines on my first boss, and the rest that followed with regards, a. Jackie.

What was your First Boss Like?

My first boss was a nun. Sr. Francis Teresa, at St Joseph's convent. (an Anglo Indian sister). She was tall and hefty, above average height and weight. I was like a 16-year-old mouse in front of her. It was my gap year of teaching soon after my high school. She was average as a principal, as long as we teachers were conscious in our jobs as teachers. Sr Francis taught me to come out of my shell (that mum sheltered and protected me while I was under her care at home). I learnt to handle a classroom of children, organize sports, games and drama, all under Sr Francis. She was good.

Coincidentally, when I took up a job in a sister convent, at St. Joseph's convent in Vizag (after my marriage, and settling in Vizag), Sr Francis' own sister (also a nun), was my principal (boss) here. She was a lovely, kind, and accommodating individual, and we got on well.

I had shuffled around with a few jobs before I settled down in marriage. This way I got to know and experience and learn a few languages of that particular state, culture and experience the different climates too. As it varied from state to state. At Ooty, I had an Australian Principal—Miss House. A fine, tall, well-mannered and well-dressed lady, who organized the school professionally with her staff. I could call her a boss. At Yercaud—Montfort school, ---it was brother Anslem—a jovial, well-spoken and sociable Principal.

In Dubai, again a convent. St Mary's School, where I had Sr. Fosca as my principal. Only one of my many bosses who was unfair in many ways. She was partial with the 'white' staff members, while the non-whites' like many of us Indians were not given much consideration and priority. Finally, after 12 years of working under Sr. Fosca, I decided to become my own 'Boss' in being a principal in my own school Hope Montessori, in Dubai. My staff were my family. I treated them all equally, and made each one of them feel important, happy and special, which made me an exceptionally satisfied and a happy boss. If the boss is fair, treating her staff equally and without favouritism or discrimination, make sure you will get the best performance and cooperation out of them.

.

Who is the wisest person you've known? What have you learned from them?

Who is the wisest person you have known Wisdom is knowledge to do the right thing at the right time. A wise man doesn't have to be rich or talented. A wise man follows his instincts and intuition to think wisely before committing himself to his thoughts and actions. A wise man cannot combine his wisdom with wealth. But he could attain wealth with his wisdom.

My maternal grandfather was termed as a wise man in the family. But we didn't consider him that way since he was a scrooge. He made his wealth by being wise in many ways, but using his wealth wisely and generously would've given him a nicer title of a wise man. But it didn't.

Fortunately, he passed down his wisdom to his daughter, my mother—minus his miserly ways. My mother was wise, considerate, charitable, loving and approachable, unlike my grandfather. Being wise and caring, she did for us—what made us what we her children are. Though she was an extremely strict and controlling mother—I take it, that's what made us 8 children what it turned us out to be. Though poorly off financially, she managed the family wisely and lovingly, especially to see that we had a minimum education that would take care of us in our future.

The world is full of wise men and women who have achieved much in life. Some of them can be included as my teachers who directed me in my path of education. But for me, my mum was the epitome of wisdom to us in the family.

Tell us the story of your miraculous birth

After a long break, just getting there.

The Story of my miraculous birth

Each mother has her own specific experiences during childbirth. Be it the first or the tenth pregnancy, each birth has its own explicit, characteristic effects, and gradual manner of events during this process. To be able to conceive, carry and deliver a healthy baby is the greatest gift a mother could be blessed with. Motherhood is absolutely the most wonderful title a lady could achieve on this earth.

When my mum had just missed her monthly periods, and presumed she had conceived a child, she had all the premonition and facts that it was going to be another child. I was the 5th born by birth, but 4th in consecutive number in line of her children, as mum lost her 2nd son during birth. And by now was quite well aware that she was carrying yet another child. At this juncture, with the exception of dad, no one else knew that mum was pregnant.

During one of those days when I was just a teeny-weeny tadpole inside mum, with no visible signs at all, she once had a visitor. It was afternoon time, when a moderately old man opened the latch of our driveway gate (we had no car), and walked in to reach the entrance of the porch. He called out for attention, and mum came from inside. He was holding a little cloth bundle under his arm. Mum, watching this someone walking in, was curious to know who he was, and went forward to greet him with courtesy. As always, mum was ready to welcome and help anyone in need. As he came forward and halted at the porch, mum asked him what he would like to have coffee, tea, etc. He was pleased to notice mum's mannerism, her kindness, and her charitable gestures. He expressed to her that he just wanted to rest for a little while, as he's been on the road walking for quite some time, and was knocked out tired. There were two parapets on either side of the entrance of our porch, so she let him rest on one of them, and went about her business inside the house.

After an hour or two, she came to the porch to check on the ole guy, who was just waking up from is deep slumber, feeling a lot more relaxed, stronger and agile, as the weakness had vanished, and he now felt refreshed, and was ready for a cup of tea, which mum gladly prepared and gave him. While accepting the tea, he gave mum a thrusting stare, and predicted her pregnancy by saying "I can say you're pregnant, this is going to be a very serious, and dangerous childbirth that you will be having. It will be a premature delivery. But I can help you if you will believe and trust in me". So, mum enquired what she should do about it, and how he was going to help. He immediately opened his little bundle, and gave mum this elixir in the form of some powder, wrapped carefully in a small piece of newspaper. He advised/instructed mum to mix a portion of it in Holy water and have it during her labour moments, which will start much earlier than the fulfilled period of pregnancy. Mum didn't take these statements seriously at all. She thought it was just another palm reader predicting something. But she was shocked to assume that the old guy had predicted her pregnancy, when in reality just dad knew the fact that mum was pregnant. He also told mum to name the baby Thomas if he was a boy, and Maria if she was a girl (my second name is Maria), and after a few moments, he was gone.

After he left, mum found a small dark blue (milk of magnesia) bottle, and emptied the powder into it. She left it on the altar and had completely forgotten about it.

Mum's pregnancy with me was advancing smoothly. Finally, when the 8th month dawned, she suddenly began to feel uncomfortable, something like the previous labour pains started. All 7 of us (with the exception of Rency the youngest) were born at home under the supervision, guidance, and timely help from the midwife. Mum's pains increased, and the same midwife was called for. She came surprisingly, as she knew it was not the time for mum's delivery. Checked mum's status, and said she was in the 8th month, and in labour, and that it looked like a serious, and dangerous delivery. She did an internal examination and found that the baby had not yet turned to position of delivery, and was still in a breech position (with the legs down and head up) since the child was in a premature state.

There was chaos in the house (still a hospital delivery was not even suggested). A lot of candles were lit on the altar, as a prayer group including my 9-year-old brother Brian, knelt down and started special prayers for mum's and baby's safety. Someone ran to call a doctor, as the midwife couldn't take the baby out, due to the breech position, though mum cooperated a lot.

From where mum was positioned in her room, she could hear a lot of prayers being said, and could see a part of the altar too from where she lay. All at once she saw the small blue bottle on the altar (containing the powder given by the old visitor 7 months ago). Mum requested dad to get the bottle from the altar, pour in some Holy water, shake it and give her a dose of it. Dad did accordingly. No longer did mum take a portion of this miraculous potion, the baby automatically turned inside her womb to the right position of head down, and mum got ready for the position of giving birth. With a lot of help from the midwife, the birth took place, bringing forth a beautiful baby girl (so said mum). She was just about 8 months old, small, premature, not crying, and with eyes closed, and stayed so for 3 days. Noticing that the baby wasn't opening her eyes, after 3 days she was taken to a doctor, who predicted that the baby would have lost her eyesight, had mum delayed by a single day to visit the doctor.

Well, that little premature, breach child was me. Born miraculously. Mum recollected that the old man with the miraculous potion was no other than St Thomas, who was one of the saints that visited and died in India in 72 AD, and was buried in Thomas Cathedral, in Mylapore, Madras. Mum concluded this since he requested mum to name the baby Thomas if he was born a boy.

The talk of the miraculous potion spread like wildfire in Cochin. One of mum's neighbour girls who was in labour for three days came to know of the miraculous medicine that helped mum deliver me. They humbly requested mum for the rest of the blessed potion she had. Mum generously gave this to the girl in long labour. Like how the blessed potion helped mum to deliver me safely, the girl who drank the potion too delivered her baby as soon as she drank this. Mum believed that the miraculous potion given to her was by St Thomas.

After mum told me this story, I asked her, "mummy, couldn't you have saved this great miraculous potion for us your daughters, when the time came for our deliveries, it would have eased us a lot of pain'. But instead, she prayed for us from the time of conception till their safe deliveries. And so God and His mother helped each of mum's four daughters to conceive, carry, and deliver healthy normal children to full term, since all four of us, as well as mum's daughters in law lived healthy lives and stayed healthy in order to produce healthy children."

Where is your secret garden where you live?

Attaching My Secret Garden.

This resort type of community living where I live in Bangalore, called Prestige Tranquility, is just what I dreamed of as a home, after my retirement, from working abroad for 33 years. I only had an artist's view of the whole picture at the time of investing in 2012. But that picture in a blue print captured my heart. The greenery and landscapes., flowering trees and plants looked breathtaking for a settlement place in India.

After retiring from managing my own school in Dubai, we got fully transferred to this beautiful dreamland on May 5th, 201, Prestige Tranquility (the very name made me feel I was investing rightly), massive 50 acres plot of land far away far

from the city chaos and crowds, just what I preferred after my years living in a concrete jungle of Dubai.

Most of the land was given for greenery, with large exotic flowering trees, dates and palm trees, and thousands of beautiful rare plants with colourful flowers, creepers and bushes, borders, shrubs, including a large number of coconut and other fruit trees.

I couldn't have asked for a more heavenly landscape city in a city. The beautiful, colourful, meandering jogging paths and sit out gardens fascinated me too.

Every morning, I enjoyed my regular walks among these beautiful trees loaded with colourful flowers according to their seasons. A beautiful sight to see colourful birds chirping, squirrels squeaking, finding their way up and down trees and across lawns, and the colourful butterflies and bees fluttering around flowers, and occasionally resting on them to suck up some nectar from a few of those beautiful flowers in the sunshine. My horticulturist interest grew, and I became a member of the horticulturist group for suggestions and ideas, which kept me interestingly occupied in my very own vicinity.

In the midst of this paradise, I found pleasure in creating my secret garden. It started with a lemon tree that I noticed was fully bloomed with fragrant white flowers. It was far away from

the jogging or normally walking paths, as I accidently discovered the lemon tree. As days and months went by, the lemons came on slowly. And after about 3 months, the tree was filled with seasoned lemons. An enriching, heavenly smell that surrounded the tree, and so far not noticed by anyone else. I plucked a few to my satisfaction and happiness.

With the help and permission, the horticulturist, I started preparing the area to add more plants to this newly discovered Secret Garden. Soon I planted potatoes, tomatoes, beetroot, pineapple, and a few other root veggies. I revealed the secret of my garden to my gardener, who gladly helped me and encouraged me with my little project that I visited and watered every morning. MY HAPPINESS!!

What was it like to move to Dubai from India? How did that happen and what was life there like?

This is the last of the topics that was given to me and I have succeeded in completing it.

What was it like to move to Dubai from India

In 1978, when my first born son, Lloyd was just about two and half years old, and I was expecting my second son Andre, mum came down to help me with my to-be-born, as well as enjoy some quality time with me, and my little family in Vizag.

It was during this time when Lionel's sister Colleen, who was already settled in Oz for a few years now, invited Lionel and his little family to join her in Oz for a better future for us. She sent

us the immigration papers for Oz, and requested Lionel to just fill up the forms and send it to her. There was no money or biometrics involved then (44 years ago). Just signatures of the applicants.

Lionel received the papers, but showed no inclination to fill it, nor had he any interest to migrate. The reason for which is still a blank question mark to me.

After about 2 weeks, mum and I approached Lionel about filling up the forms as, the sooner it was sent, the better future for our family. But unfortunately, Lionel made it clear to us that he didn't want to fill the forms, nor migrate to Australia. Time was slowly moving by, and Lionel did not change his mind. He had decided not to migrate to Oz, and that was it. Mum and I practically begged him, telling him 'at least think of the children's future'. But no coaxing, or begging or requesting could change his mind. He was stubborn as a mule not to change his mind from what he had decided.

After a few months, Andre was born. Mum stayed on for about a month more, taking care of me and the baby, and again requesting Lionel to fill up the Oz papers for our future benefit. Finally, it was time for mum to return to Cochin, where mum and dad were stationed at that time.

After a few months had gone by, Lamby sent Lionel a letter (we had no phones then), asking him if he was interested in going to Dubai to start a new life, job, etc. By now few of my siblings were already in Dubai, and working. Lionel showed interest in going to Dubai, and took this opportunity. Though I repeatedly reminded him it would be beneficial moving to Oz for a permanent settlement with the family, than going to Dubai where one day we have to get back to India when we retire in Dubai. Anyway, going to Dubai would any day be better than staying back in India for the future.

Hence Lionel made plans to leave for Dubai in July 1979. And he left, much against my liking.

Andre was born, and just about in his crawling stage when Lionel left for Dubai, leaving me and my two little boys alone in Vizag. I was then teaching at St. Joseph's Convent. But after a few months, I did not want to stay in Vizag anymore, so I decided to return to Cochin and stay with mum and dad and my two little boys. I slowly closed shop by getting rid of all the furniture, clothes and other household essentials, and left for Cochin by train. Just me, boys and I.

Back in Cochin where I was born and grew up, the place was not strange to me. I felt comfortable and companionable staying with mum and dad. After few months, I took up a reputable job in a premium well established Kindergarten school in the Naval Base. A few months later, Lloyde was old enough to join Kinder at the same Naval KG. So, we went and returned everyday by the public bus.

Andre was still a baby and was taken care of by mum, along with her 2 adopted boys Sathish and Rahim.

At Naval Kindergarten with Admiral Dawson

Time passed by, and after 2 years, Andre was able to join us too. It was quite tiring for me, as by the time we got back from school, the kids were sleepy. Andre had to be carried a good distance from the bus stop. Besides hugging on to Lloyd, our tiffin boxes, and my school books. But three of us spent a lot of quality time together at school, home, parks and playgrounds. We had a good rapport with each other. Mum and dad helped me overcome my emotional and physical strain.

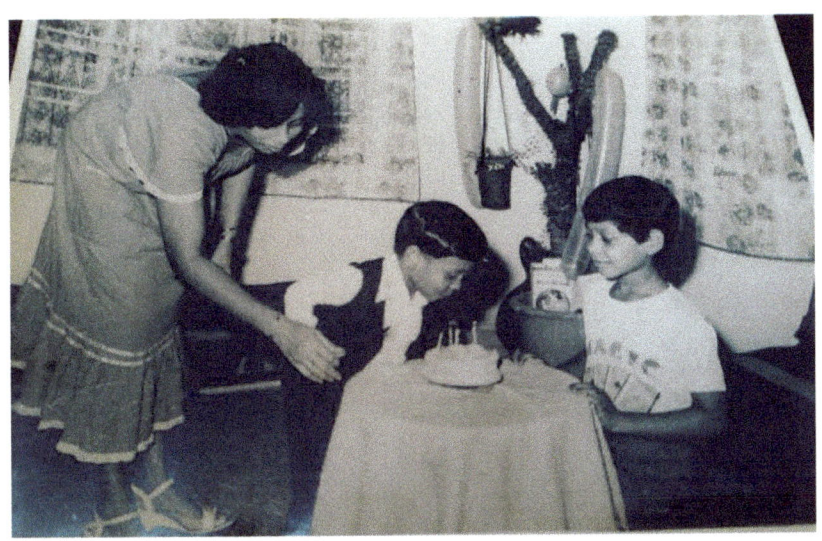

After 3 years, Lionel visited us for the first time since he left for Dubai. The relationship between the children and the father was strange, since they got to experience being with him after a long time. Time passed quickly, and after 6 years, Lionel got prepared to take the kids and me to live with him in Dubai. As then Lionel concluded that he could financially be able to give us a more comfortable life there, than in India. Besides, most importantly, we could live in Dubai as a family. Hence the boys and I joined Lionel in the peak of a hot summer on the 5th of July, 1985.

The very next day of my arrival there, Dyllis had arranged for an interview for me at St. Mary's Catholic School in Dubai. I was happily accepted and overjoyed when the principal asked me to join work when the schools reopened after the summer holidays. Meanwhile, at the interview with the headmistress, Sr. Fosca asked me if I was willing to take up a temporary job (until the schools reopened for the new term) to teach spoken English classes to the adult Arab ladies at the Zabeel palace. It was beyond imagination for me to have been chosen to teach English at the Sheik's palace. That too, the very next day after my arrival in Dubai.

Family gathering on our arrival at Dubai

On every alternate day, a limousine picked and dropped me for the English classes at the palace. I enjoyed being with the teenagers and young adult women, and most importantly to teach the women of a different nationality (compared to India), and spend time with these young adults, and a few seniors at the palace. Meanwhile, I made arrangements to register and admit Lloyd and Andre into an Indian school.

At the end of my term in the palace, towards the end of August I decided to terminate my temporary palace job, as St Mary's was reopening on 1st September. They gave me a decent package for my teaching at the palace, which helped me financially towards our new move into Dubai.

With Sister Josephine at St Mary's convent

I started school at St. Mary's on the 1st of September, and was appointed as a kindergarten teacher in charge of 35 students- all four and five year olds. Unlike India, I had a good bunch of children of different nationalities and most astonishingly, 3 princesses from the same Zabeel palace, belonging to the Sheik's family.

I enjoyed my teaching at St Mary's, except that our salaries were quite low without an increment in 5 to 8 years.

Along with St Mary's teachers

Finally, after putting in 12 years of hard work there with a meagre salary, and not being able to manage and maintain the huge expenses we were facing for the three children's education and our needs. Dyllis, my sister who was also working with me as a teacher at St.

Mary suggested a brilliant, as well as a risky idea/plan, that both of us resign from St. Mary's, and start our very own Kindergarten, Nursery school, with daycare. We shook hands, and invested our gratuity of 12 years received from St. Mary's, into our new venture Hope Montessori School, which formerly belonged to Dyllis's friend Ms. Zainab. She was by now a very sick person, having to go to the UK for treatment quite often. Hence, she couldn't manage running the school successfully anymore.

It all started on 30th June as summer classes, to begin with. By now all the schools in Dubai and other Emirates had closed for the summer break.

Learning with Montessori Apparatus

We advertised mostly by word of mouth, and distributed a few fliers to the surrounding school areas. Location was our greatest asset. A little 2 storey villa located in the midst of a commercial, business and prominent area in the heart of Dubai.

We performed excellently with extreme hard work, and interest. In a week's time, the school was overflowing with children of all age groups. Few of our teacher friends who never went on their summer break, were still in Dubai, and willing to help us handle the classes. Children were grouped in classes according to their age. This helped us segregate work and activities to suit their age group. Classes were organized with a lot of outdoor and indoor activities, art and craft, fruit, and cooking activities, etc. The children enjoyed every day of their summer camp. It was a bumper crowd of children for us, as at that time there were no summer camps organized by any other institution.

Finally, by the end of August, the summer classes came to an end, as the schools were re-opening by the first week of September, and the children had to resume their normal classes in their respective schools.

Now was the time for us to work harder, and bring in more children for our daily normal school activities, including day-care, and accepting a few babies too. Our working hours were from 7 am to 7pm, and that suited the working parents who had children to be taken care of. We employed a few more teachers and nannies as the number of children began to increase. While Dyllis and I worked as director, Principal, as nannies when required, as a nurse, PRO, purchaser, organizer, and just like this, our hard work never goes unnoticed.

We organized sports day activities, fancy dress competitions, Christmas season celebrations, graduation day presentations, parents' day gatherings, and many more. Progress card reports were prepared for each child on the school performance and behaviour. Parents were immensely impressed with the way we went about organizing the school, and activities using Montessori apparatus, which inculcate good manners, and the use of day to day house training using mats, brooms, spades, pans, measuring cups etc. Our school flourished with word of mouth good impressions of our school from the parents.

With the HMS teachers Graduation Day at HMS

Every morning school activities commenced with a long assembly of all the children, and teachers, and the principal taking part in songs, rhymes and action songs accompanied by music played by a professional musician.

HMS, in abbreviation of Hope Montessori School, grew and grew and grew from 9 children and a teacher initially, to 260 children, and 23 staff members, a doctor on call and a full time nurse.

In course of time, Dyllis started her own school quite a distance away from HMS. But our close friendship and agreement to our contract remained unaltered. I was given a salary to manage the school myself with my existing staff, who were all so loyal, dedicated, hardworking, and respectful.

Since Dyllis and I were now managing separate schools, we had so much news to share with each other during the weekend, when we joined every Thursday at the British club for dinner and a glass of wine. Long chats that we looked forward to every weekend.

Initially, I sponsored mum to Dubai from Bangalore, since most of her children were now in Dubai with their families. After a year or two when it was time to renew mum's visa, Lambert decided to transfer mum's sponsorship to his care, while deciding to keep mum fully at his place after he and his family moved to a bigger bungalow. Mum was provided with maids and a caregiver. She felt quite comfortable at Lamby's place. There was a large garden, open spaces as well as useful trees. Mum loved to be wheeled in there during the cool evenings. Most friday evenings, the majority of the family joined in at Lamby's to spend a few quality hours with mum, thereby treating us with grand dinners organized by Lamby and his wife Dianne. We have unforgettable memories of lovely times, dinners and get-togethers here at Lamby's place in Sharjah.

All our children grew up well, graduated at well-known colleges/universities, and remained good as long as we parents molded them accordingly.

Dubai has been our home for many years, where we had so many memorable celebrations with our family members and friends. Few of us had our own establishments as well, which brought in good income for the concerned families. Our children settled in good jobs, and we were happy about it. Slowly, few of the family members decided to build their permanent nest abroad in places like Canada, Australia, the US, and Singapore. In course of time, a lot of them were disappearing to greener pastures. Lionel and I had no other alternative but to return to India for settlement. While our children decided to continue working in Dubai as long as it allowed them to.

Since my final destination was going to be India, I volunteered to keep mum and take care of her till her last day. Lamby was now getting ready to shift to Canada, but he financed mum's care, though she was with me in presence. By now mum had gotten into

Alzheimer's fully, and was not aware where she was. Finally on the 12th of April 2014, mum said 'goodbye' to all of us in my home in Bangalore. That was an end to a grand era.

Some memorable events in Dubai

Mum's and dad's Golden wedding on the 19th of May 1987.

Mum's memorable birthdays celebrated every year with pomp and show at Lamby's place

My daughter (Anna's) birth after a gap of 10 years.

Few important weddings of the family members took place in Dubai (one of which was Karl's).

My children's Lloyd and Anna's weddings,

and me fulfilling my desire of travelling the world over, mostly with Lloyd providing us with our flight tickets.

Our Silver Wedding crowd in Dubai

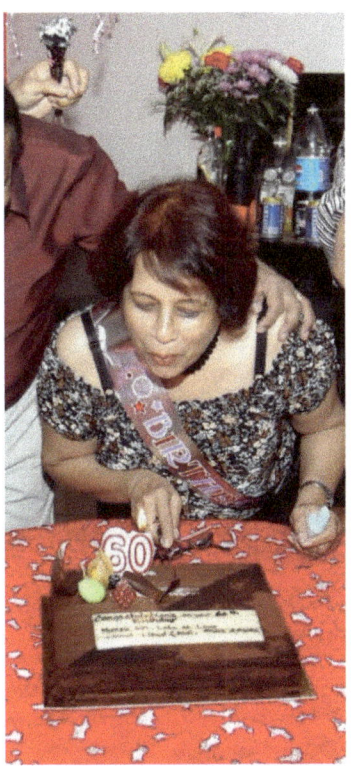

My 60th Birthday in Dubai

Dates in Dubai

On an Emirates Flight to USA fulfilling my desires of travelling the world

Which people have been the kindest to you in life?

The Kindest People in my Life.

Which people have been the kindest to you in life?

I can point out to 4 dear people who have been the kindest to me in life.

Considering my arrogance, demanding and abrupt nature, I look up to these people who have forgiven my sometimes atrocious behaviour, and have taken me under their protection.

Starting with my dearest father– Daddy Jackson was one of the kindest, mildest, and the most patient father I have ever heard of. During my lifetime, dad I was never once reprimanded, scolded or punished. Nor were the rest of my siblings. We never heard him shout or scream, as mum did the controlling part. Dad was a very decent human being, highly respected by all of us. He didn't have a high position in life, nor at his job. But with his meagre salary, all of the 8 children were fed and educated. Dad was very mild and kind in his ways. He cried bitterly on my wedding day, as I was leaving home to be with my husband in another state of India. We were very close to each other, until dad passed away at the age of 78 in 1989.

When I was just about 22 years, and a teacher at Montfort Boys High school, Brother Wilfred who was in his late 40's and the treasurer of the school, was the best liked brother in the whole school, by the boys and staff members. I soon began to take a special liking to him, and later realized why I did so. He reminded me of the qualities of my father. I gathered that brother Wilfred was the kindest, most down to earth, non-materialistic, honest, and always wanting to give, and impart kindness, not only to me, but to everyone who knew him. Brother did the best he could for the benefit of the school, the boys as well as the staff.

Even after I left the school, got married, and settled down in another state to start my family, we kept in touch with snail mail letters, wishing each other on special occasions etc.

After I got back to India on retirement, leaving my working enterprises abroad, I made it a point to visit brother Wilfred in Yercaud, whenever it was convenient for me, as it's just a 7 hours ride from where I am located at the moment in Bangalore. Brother is also retired now and lives with the other retired brothers, at Louis Villa Montfort. He has always opened the doors of generosity to me, for my staying and boarding at Louis vills each time I visited him. The last I visited him was for his 95th birthday on 12th Feb 2021. Even at this age, he recognizes me and speaks in a kind and generous way, always showering me with gifts (given to him by other friends like me). I pray that God continues to keep him in good health and kindness.

My next dear person who has been good and kind and forgiving to me in spite of my sometimes rudeness, my selfishness, and my unforgiving ways at times, is my dear darling first born son Lloyd. Always so loving, kind, forgiving, appreciative, and generous and helpful in his ways. This way we created a solid bond. A rock of love, care, and togetherness. He understands and forgives my faults as no one else could.

And finally, my very dear sister Dyllis, who has always stood by me during my highs and lows, good times and bad. She is and always will be my best friend as long as I live.

We caught up together studying in the same class from grade 9. We did high school together, trained as teachers together, got married to our partners with just a gap of 6 months difference, had our first born around the same time and were teaching together in the same schools. Until we started our own school as partners (in Dubai). We did well, cooperate with each other, and managed the school successfully. Generating a substantial sum of money for our present retired life. But it saddens me now that we're living poles apart, and not able to meet each other as frequently as before. She is settled in Sydney, Australia, while I live here in Bangalore, India. The best way we communicate with each other now is by speaking for 2 hours with each other every Thursday on WhatsApp.

What's the first major news story you can remember living through as a child?

With a lot of difficulty, I'm sending you this story. I will send the rest in course of time, as I'm still laid up. sorry for the delay. A. Jackie

The first major news story I can remember living through as a child.

The earliest shocking and the saddest memory I have had as a child was of the assassination of a real great, and well-loved American President, our dear President John F. Kennedy. I was just 12 years old, but somehow admired him as a good, kind and handsome young, catholic president. He was quite popular and well-known. John was from a noble family, and his ancestors were from a political field. He was my idol even before I was a teenager.

His famous quote was, "don't ask what America can do for you, ask what you can do for America".

He was famously known for his success in the famous Cuba crisis against Russia.

John had a beautiful wife, Jacqueline, also known as Jackie Kennedy, and 2 young beautiful children, Caroline and John Jr.

It was on 22nd November 1963, when I was with a group of friends, we got the sudden, saddening news of President John Kennedy's assassination, which shockingly happened while John and Jackie were touring Dallas in their official open car, on an official state visit. He was shot near Dealey Plaza by an American US Veteran Lee Harvey Oswald.

This was the very first piece of sad news for me at the age of 12, as President Kennedy had a special place in my heart.

Coincidently, 8 years ago, I had decided to travel around the US with the intention of visiting a lot of places in America, my most liked and loved country, along with my husband Lionel. Starting with Texas, we visited many famous states where country and

western music originated. We visited a vast area of central, western, and eastern America. And most importantly, we went close to the spot where President John Kennedy was assassinated near Dealey Plaza, in Dallas. We took pictures of that spot he was shot in his car (marked with a cross). I saw the spot where my idol was killed. I accepted it as a sad sight. John is and always was my most favourite of all the US presidents till date.

Knocking on Heavens Door

Knocking on Heaven's door

Lionel and I celebrated a memorable Christmas in 2021 with a couple friends, Patricia & Walter who came in from Goa, and stayed over to spend Christmas and a few more days here with us. After the wonderful get together, they left back on the 28th. That same night, I felt a bit extra tired, and developed a back pain. Just consider it as a side effect of an overworked weekend. Hence, I got into bed to rest. No pain killer helped me. I spent the night with a lot of pain and discomfort, added with chills. I couldn't sleep. Around 6.30 am, on the 29th, the back pain had developed into a painful, intolerable, unable to accept situation, which made it uncomfortable for me to stand, sit or even lie down. I asked one of the youngsters in our tower to call for our community ambulance, which arrived in no time, and took me to the nearest best hospital… Manipal Hospital.

I was taken into emergency, from where quick proceedings took place with MRT scans, x rays, blood tests, etc, for my back. The tests showed no signs of emergency for the excruciating pain in my back after reading all the tests. So, the doctor asked me if I had any other existing problem, which could have led to the back pain. I told the doctor that I have had knee arthritis for quite many years now, and was managing the discomfort with painkillers, gels and the like. So, they decided to do an arthroscopy of the knee, and value its readings. By doing so and valuing the tests, the doctor concluded that I had septic arthritis, which has caused severe infection in my leg and surrounding areas, and my life would be threatened, unless an emergency operation was done on the knee with continued medical procedures and strong medications.

I was admitted to the hospital for an emergency knee operation. My problem was termed as septicemia, which was initially caused by urinary tract infection. A normal count of infection (CRP) for a person is around 5, while mine was 358. And nearly on the point of death, if the infection had spread throughout my system and attacked my organs, the doctor said I had only a 1 % survival rate of survival. I was starting on a perilous journey with no sight of the future... except PRAYERS.

My back pain had come from nowhere as a disguise to hurry me to the hospital on time, to save my life.

The very next day, an emergency operation was done on my left knee to remove part of the infection which had attacked my arthritic knee via a UTI, which was not obvious to me in any form.

After an anesthetic operation and 16 stitches on my knee, I was brought back to my room (we had requested for a double room, so that Lionel could stay in too). From then on, I was pumped with high doses of intravenous antibiotics, pain killers, saline, blood transfusions, etc. When the sedatives got worn off, I was in my height of pain and agony. I was constantly monitored by doctors and nurses. The highly strong medications started draining my appetite. Hence, food intake became minimal and my haemoglobin began to drop drastically. I became very weak, and gradually couldn't consume anything at all except a whole load of medicines. Pain killers were constantly infused intravenously. This went on for 2 weeks, added with blood transfusions. After 4 days, the physiotherapists came to help me take a few steps with the walker. It was a whole load of pain after pain for me.

On the 10th day, the Ortho doctor decided for me to leave the hospital, but continue with the IV's and physiotherapy at home. My appetite continued to drop, and so did my haemoglobin. But with blood tests every 3 to 4 days, we were relieved to see the CRP counts dropping to a tolerable level, mostly due to the strong antibiotics that were being taken intravenously. My most precious angel who helped me

In Manipal Hospital

Lloyd rubbing my legs with oil Bouquet of get well wishes from Dyllis

Finally, on the 16th day after the surgery, and with the stitches still on, I came home in an ambulance on 12th Jan. Fortunately, for me, I had contacted a house nurse agency who provided me with a 24 hours care giver, and we were able to bring her home in the same ambulance.

Fatima, my caregiver, and Lionel mostly, began to give me 100%care, love, and concern. My appetite continued to drop. Intravenous meds continued at home with the help of our clinic nurses. I became very weak, losing 10 ½ kgs in 1 ½ months. There was nothing on this earth that I ever had a liking to consume. Anything forcibly would be brought out. I was given medication for appetite as well as to retain my intake. But nothing seemed to help, except prayers from the family and around.

Finally, around the end of January, I knocked on Heaven's Door (I had no physical strength or energy). Heaven's door wasn't opening for me. Instead, God sent lots of Angels to help me. I can name those angels.... Most importantly, Lionel my husband who

was by my side 24 hours of the day and night. And professional angels Dr. Dev, Dr. Sushamita,and few more, who kept monitoring me every day at the hospital, and at home. More angels were the numerous nurses, and other health care staff, along with my caregiver, Fatima. But the most important, caring, and loving of all the angels, was Lionel.... Who wept with me, and prayed for me during my painful, difficult moments. Times when I could hardly move an inch of my body, nor hold the phone to message my dear siblings, (who went through anxious moments) with pains all over my body, added with a non-stop spasmodic cough, that increased more pains all over.

Lionel tried cooking for me, and even spoon feeding me in order to lift me up physically and mentally. I was just fading away. Lloyd, Andre and Anna, my loving angels, tried talking to me on the phone, and on zoom. I was so weak and lifeless that I could not respond to the children in any way. IV's were continuously being given by the Sanjiwani nurse. Nothing improved my appetite, and my weakness had reached its death point around 25th of January, when, with a lot of strain and pain, I messaged Lionel one of my photos, requesting him to use it as my obituary picture, as I was going to sleep with the lord that night. Lionel fell on the bed, held my hands and burst out in severe sobs. I couldn't help him in any way, nor could he. I tried knocking on heaven's door again, but it wasn't opening for me. God said I

need to spend some more time with my husband and children, since it was also Lionel's 80th birthday (that we celebrated in June this year). And then I dozed off for a little while. After a restless night, I woke up to see the face of my angel.... Lionel...by my side, clutching my hand. God said to me, "I don't want you now, go to your husband, he can't survive without you. Be strong, you will be on the path to wellness soon." My girl Fatima was another angel who cared for me immensely.

After two more weeks of blood transfusions and medications, there was a respite when the IV's were concluded, and replaced with lighter doses of medications. This awakened my appetite a bit and I was beginning to accept liquids without bringing them out. I began to regain my strength slowly after mid-March, when my boys promised to come down and spend a few days with me for my birthday, at the end of March. By then, the covid situation had weakened too, and the flights were opening up. This brought about a huge difference in me mentally as well as physically. And sure as the joys of heaven poured in, my boys came, bringing in their love and warmth to improve my health status.

I was helped with continuous physiotherapy every evening. Except for the walking part (most of the time in a wheelchair or stick), I was beginning to recoup my strength slowly. I was trying to lie less in bed, and spend more time sitting on a couch. My

biggest concern was I couldn't continue with my story writing, as I was unable to hold a pen, or handle the computer keyboard, nor sit up straight on a chair.

My angels, Lionel and the boys pumped in a lot of life concerns, and the importance of positive living. It did boost me with their presence here with me on my birthday in March. They left at the end of March, promising to take Lionel and me to Dubai by the 1st week of June. Yes, and they did keep their promise. They arranged luxury flights for us, and a grand holiday for us in different parts of the UAE from the 2nd of June to the 15th of June, in celebration for Lionel's 80th birthday, and our 48th wedding anniversary, as both the special occasions fell during this time while we were there with the children.

Happy reunion with our children on Lionel's 80th and our 43rd

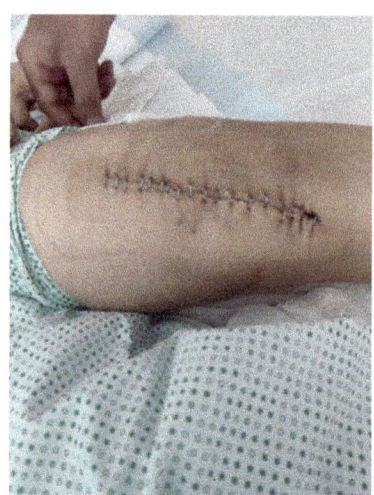

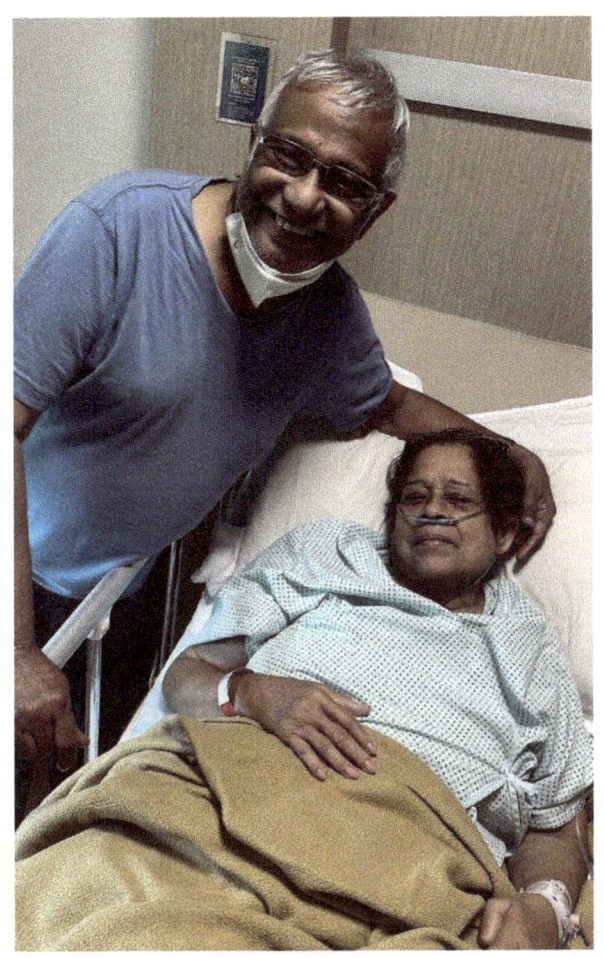

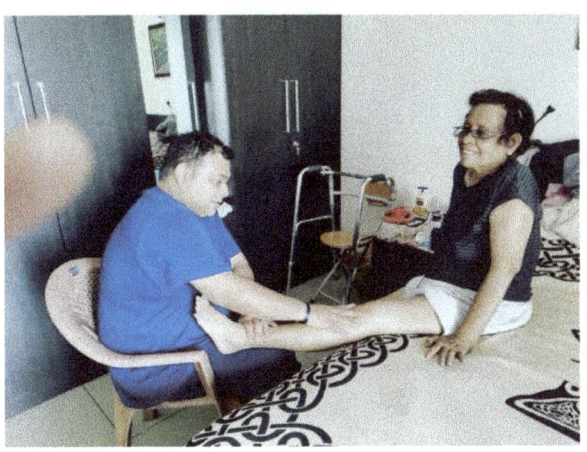

Would you prefer to have an adventure, or read about one?

Attaching would you like to prefer an Adventure or Read about one.

Would you prefer to experience an adventure or read about one Sure, I would love to experience and enjoy adventures, as well as read about them.

One of the most amusing as well as dangerously adventurous trips I had was, when we wanted to mount a horse and go for a ride through a stretch of mud and slushy paths (where no automobile ventured) in Shimla (N India). While mounting the horse, it took me for a spin, and I was thrown down, my bag and all. Unfortunately, there was no one around to click a picture of that. And fortunately enough, I didn't get hurt. But later on, I got a picture on the horse.

The second adventure was when Lionel (my husband) and I wanted to go for a ride on a mountain buffalo in Kashmir. That was interesting, as the buffaloes were tame, and we went for a calm and jolly ride.

What are some of your pet peeves?

Sorry I have not had any interest in pets. Jackie.

Sorry, I sent the wrong message in regards to pet peeves. Will get back.

A peeve is an annoyance, and a pet peeve is an annoyance that's nurtured like a pet. It's something someone can never resist. It's a frequent subject of complaint. Pet peeve is something that annoys or bothers a person very much. A behaviour or display that generates annoyance in certain people.

Everybody is wired differently. What might seem completely harmless to one, can be very annoying to someone else. It can be termed as an OCD (Obstructive compulsive disorder).

For example, maybe I can get antsy when my husband (Lionel) sometimes comes into the kitchen to do some of his own cooking, and leaves a mess around. Loud music is a pet peeve for me. In fact, I have many peeves. An untidy kitchen or unkempt toilet, an unorganized study table or drawers, vessels not washed well, bed not well made, towels not well folded on the stand, etc.

OCD's always find fault with non OCD's ways of doing things, or in arrangements.

I'll end my story by saying that I have umpteen pet peeves.

What were your favorite subjects in high school?

There were subjects I didn't show much interest in while at school, but I had no other option other than to study. But there were 2 favourite subjects that interested me. English literature, grammar, and geography. Our 2nd language was a compulsory subject... Malayalam, the local language. But I made an efficient, strong and determined effort to master the language. So much so, I scored well in the subject, and can even now read and write it.

Geography was quite interesting. Hence, I took an interest to personally learn and experience a lot of geographical emphasis from different parts of the world. Thereby, traveling internationally and intensely, and learning the physical features, climate, culture, language, currency and many more features of different parts of the world.

What are some of your family traditions?

To begin with, most importantly, we, the whole family take part in our daily rosary, and other important prayers said/recited by the elders, usually between 6 and 7 pm every day.

On Christmas day, all 8 children, mum and dad joined together on a large mat to have our special Christmas meal, after initially attending the Christmas mass together. It was the same for Easter celebrations. During Christmas week, we visited most of our relatives, to wish them for the special season.

Traditionally, all of us got a new outfit along with a custom pair of shoes for the occasion. We didn't have any gifts to open on Christmas day, nor for our birthdays, as money didn't come in easily for us, with just dad as a working member of a large family of 10 members.

Mum made cake and wine, besides a few of the famous Christmas sweets, which we distributed among relatives and friends.

That was it from what I can remember.

What fascinated you as a child?

To begin with, as a child, I was always fascinated playing with boys of my age, and all their games. Like flying kites, spinning tops, marbles, and balls, etc. I was termed as a Tomboy. I never liked playing with dolls and girlie stuff. I had a great fascination in collecting stamps from all over the world. So, my little pocket money was always spent on stamps. One of my brothers who always travelled the world as a shipper, sent me stamps from different countries he visited, and my interest in them grew. I spent a lot of my time mounting them in stamp books.

I had thousands of them from various countries of the world. It was my precious possession, until I had my first son, and found less and less time to spend on my stamp collection, and so quite conveniently passed on my precious hobby to my husband, Lionel, who took over with genuine interest.

Another thing that fascinated me from young till the age of 18 or 19 was to climb trees. Which proved that I was a tomboy. I loved climbing any tree at all, be it a mango tree or even coconut trees. But the tree climbing came to an end after I got married, and shifted to another state, living in a place that had no trees anywhere around.

My childhood was innocently spent, until I decided to get married and settle down with my husband.

How far back can you trace your family ancestry?

Being born an Anglo Indian, I know for sure that my ancestors were European settlers who came to India for trade and settlement in the 18th century. They Intermarried with the Indians, to eventually create us Anglo Indians, now a small minority of this community left back in India, while majority of them traced back their origins in Europe, and otherwise found greener pastures in Australia, England, Canada, and America.

My dad's grandfather was an English man by the name of Jackson. His son Wilfred was my dad Nelson's father. But I didn't get to see my grandfather or grandmother on my father's side, as my dad lost his mother (to jaundice) while he was just 90 days old, and his father too died young even before I grew up.

The ancestral story seems to be a little longer on my mum's side, since mum lived to the ripe old age of few months short of completing 100 years. Her memory and speech were sharp and accurate till the age of 96, after which Alzheimer's set in. During her sharp memory days, she narrated a lot of family facts, which interested us children, knowing little that I would someday put it all down in writing, like what I'm doing now.

Mum's father was Peter Furtal, who married my grandmother Mary when she was just 13 years old. In the bygone days, all they wanted from a woman was to produce children and take care of the house, while the men were their bosses who worked and provided for the family. Peter Furtal was a well acclaimed supervisor of the TATA oil company in his home town Ernakulam, in the state of Kerala. He did well financially, attained a good name, and was a tall, rich man owning many houses and shops in and around the vicinity where he lived.

Peter's father was Micheal Furtal, a Dutch man who came to India in the late 18th century, as a spice merchant, and started his own business in spices, and later invested in the fishing business by owning a number of fishing boats in Ernakulam, and in Vallarpadam, a little coastal Village near Ernakulam in Kerala. He was an extremely rich man owning a large part of Ernakulam, under which was covered the infant Jesus church, and the Ernakulam high court. In his first marriage, he had no children, so he left her. In his 2nd marriage to Philomena, a Keralite, he had 2 boys, from which my grandfather Peter was the eldest boy, and another son by the name of Francis. He married again for the 3rd time, and had 7 daughters. One of the daughters was Theresa, whose daughter is our well known aunty Maida, who at the moment lives in Canada, and a sweetheart of a lady, so loving and kind to all of us. She helped in giving me some of this information too. She is the oldest living aunt I have on my mum's side, besides uncle Archie, papa Francis' son. It's such a joy to meet and spend some time with them. Maida. each time I visit Canada.

Tell us about your travels

That's an interesting topic!

While in my teens and growing up, we never really had opportunities or the finances, or choice of places to travel to. My first train ride was when I was 18 years old when I was going to Madras for my teacher's training studies. Later on, my sister and I chose different parts of India to go to and settle in teaching. This way we saw a lot of North and South India, its various climatic changes, cultures, traditions, grasped a little of their languages, food preferences, etc. Places like Delhi, Calcutta, Madras, Vizag, Ooty, Coonoor, Yercaud, Shimla, Bombay Jamshedpur, Kharagpur, Kerala, Goa, Pune, Orissa, etc.,etc.

National Costume of Shimla

In 1985, I had the opportunity of leaving India for Dubai on my first international flight. From then, the ball started rolling for me at a fast pace in traveling.

The very first place I visited while in Dubai, was Malaysia, when I won the 1st prize 🏆 for a cooking contest organized by Rainbow 🌈 milk. We flew to Kuala Lumpur, and then a complimentary trip to Penang, while they showered us with a lot of prizes and gifts.

My next place was my childhood cherished wish to visit Switzerland. This dream was fulfilled when my son Lloyd gave me the flight ticket for Zurich. I had arranged a tour trip to visit the whole of Switzerland for Anna and me, which lasted for 8 days. My most cherished dream has come true! One of the most beautiful, scenic countries in the world.

The interest, and urge to visit more countries started building castles in the air for me, and most fortunately, my son Lloyd made all my travelling dreams come true. I only had to air out my wishes to visit a particular place, and like Aladdin and the wonderful lamp, in other words like the magic carpet, Lloyd provided us with the flight tickets, to any part of the world where Emirates flies to, as he was eligible to (since he was working in the airlines).

Turkey and Egypt were two very historical places I enjoyed visiting, besides England, with a lot of Victorian wealth and history.

There were few places like Canada, US, and Australia that I visited at least six to seven times each, as they were family oriented visits.

There were other eastern orientation trips I took to interesting places like Singapore, Bangkok, Thailand, (Kajesthan, Russian province) Macau, Hong Kong, etc.

Memphis Tennessee, USA

Ottawa, Canada.. Justin Trudeau official building

Family in Australia

Sri Lanka, through a small island country, fascinated me with the spice and tea gardens, gems and precious stone mines.

Visiting the Holy land in Jerusalem was an incredible journey of an experience, as I got to see in real life where Jesus Christ was born and buried. A realistic, true religious personality who we read and learn about nearly every day in our Catholic religion. Israel, Jordan, Bethlehem, Jerusalem, Egypt, Haifa, Palestine, Tel Aviv, etc, were another group of old historical cities that filled me with excitement when I visited the Holy land.

Place where Jesus had His agony in the garden under the olive trees

Tel Aviv Garden - one of the biggest in Israel

The spot where Jesus was crucified has become very sacred to the tourists now at the Church of Sapulpa

One other interesting place I wanted to visit in India was Kashmir. The place of natural beauty with its famous snowcapped mountain ranges (including Mount Everest), river valleys, famous fruit, and flower gardens are always in bloom. On the political side of it, millions of soldiers have lost their lives on the border, due to the long standing conflict for this Dreamland Kashmir, by India and Pakistan. I made my dream come true to see this wonderful place Kashmir just four years ago.

BetaabBetaab Valley, Kashmir

Besides my flight and land travels, I also enjoyed 2 luxurious cruises to various Eastern countries (gifted by Lloyd on our 35th wedding anniversary), and another one around the gulf waters, visiting Muscat, Abu Dhabi and Dubai.

203 | *The History of a Legend*

On Star Cruises

While in Singapore my travels have been great experiences.

Do you have any interests?

I was just 7 years old, when, one day one of my little boyfriends gave me a postage stamp. The picture on the stamp was a rocket going up into space, and it was written "Dubai" beneath the rocket . That name was an unknown word to us. I looked up the Atlas world map for Dubai. It wasn't there. I asked and enquired from many elders about where Dubai was, but no one could help me. Anyway, I decided to keep the stamp, and that was the beginning of my interest in stamp collection. Every single penny in pocket money would go into buying stamps. The more I collected, the more interest I got in stamps. My brother Willo, a shippie guy, encouraged my stamp collection interests, by posting me stamps from whichever country he visited during his voyages. Finally, it was a well-known fact that Jackie was a stamp collector in the family. A lot of my friends and family started gifting me with stamps. I began exchanging stamps with friends who had parts of the same type. By now I had a very good collection, that I got a stamp book and started mounting them there in which way they would all be safe. By the time I finished high school I had a really good collection. I began to buy some wonderful rare stamps, as well as keep a stack of mint stamps in another book. I had the gold mint album too. Lionel noticed my interest in stamps and encouraged me with stamp gifts.

After my first born Lloyd was born, spare time became less and less. So I asked Lionel if he could continue with my interest in stamps and maintain my albums. He gladly accepted the offer, and began to increase the collection with more and more stamps. He got interested in the hobby too. That's it with my stamps. The most interesting episode is......that Dubai turned out to be my second home years later, where my family and I spent 35 years in this place, where my daughter was also born. I had my own school there, and made my life time savings in this very own luxurious country, Dubai.

Another interest of mine has been, and still is... Cooking. I began to show interest in cooking from the age of 12. Often I watched my mum cooking for the family, and took some tips from her. I tried my hands at simple basic cooking, by helping my mum. She noticed my interest and often encouraged me. There was a large gap in my cooking interest after I finished my high school and left home for my further studies, and teaching. Wherein I was put up in hostels.

I rediscovered my passion for cooking after I got into Dubai, where all kinds of condiments and spices were easily available unlike in India while I was younger. I started cooking initially for my young family, and from there my cooking interests developed at a fast pace, to an extent that it encouraged me to take part in cookery contests. I started experimenting on all kinds of cooking, initially using cookery books. Like Chinese, Indian, Italian, Continental and more. Besides, trying my hands in pickles and various desserts. I began to win prizes at cookery contests like hampers, milk products, kitchen weighing gadgets, etc. The best award ever was the 1st prize for preparing a seafood saffron soup, by entering the Rainbow milk cooking contest. The prize award was a pair of flight tickets for me and my husband to Kuala Lumpur, with a 5 nights stay at a 5-star hotel Shangri-La. Also an internal flight for 2 days stay in Penang with meals and full accommodation. I continually got prizes in my favourite interest of cooking. Finally, it began to slow down after I returned to India.

My third and final interest is and always will be in gardening. This started at a very early age of 12 years, when I used to grow roses to begin with, in my little compound garden in Cochin. I had to put it on hold again during my hostel days.

Going to Dubai and continuing with gardening wasn't possible, as, first and foremost the extremely hot climate was discouraging to even think of gardening. Besides living in a flat didn't interest me to grow much, except keep few potted plants like Aloe Vera, 🌵 cactus type plants, money plants, etc .

When I got back to India about 10 years ago, I came to live in the Garden City of India, Bangalore, where the climate and soil contents are both excellent for the plants and trees.

I established my home in Prestige Tranquility, a paradise filled with thousands of flowering trees, and plants. I joined the horticulture group as a committee member for suggestions and improvements on our greenery and landscape. Even here I'm living in a flat, so I couldn't grow much on my balcony. In Spite of it, I sprouted from seed different kinds of salad leaves, curry leaves, succulents, cacti, the ZZ plants, chilies, herbs like the thyme and rosemary, tomatoes and a lot more. But my urge to vasten my horizon in plants and trees kept growing. Living within a community, this is not possible, unless I had my own piece of at least a square area of land. But fortunately for me, my wishes were granted.

During one of our regular meetings with the horticulturist and garden supervisors, I requested them for a small piece of garden area in a quiet corner of our large 40 acre land in our premises.

They gladly accepted my request (considering my age and interest in gardening). On condition I take all responsibility to care for my personal plants. I was on top of the moon with enthusiasm and joy to maintain my very own secret garden, far from the probing eyes 👀 of the rest of the people in the community. The patch already had a lemon 🍋 the tree fully bloomed with lemon flowers and hundreds of lemons. One day we got it all cleared of weeds and stones. The soil was tilled, and treated with fresh manure and compost. I began planting saplings of vegetables and fruits, like onion leeks, potatoes, root vegetables, pineapple, beans, tomatoes, and a lot more. They were all growing well, due to the climatic and soil conditions.

In course of time, the lemons grew and were seasoned enough for picking.

Then all of a sudden, I got into an emergency health situation, and was hospitalized. Hence my little secret garden, as well as my balcony garden got neglected. I was just coming out of all my trauma and beginning to regain my health, hoping to continue with my gardening and cooking in the course of time.

What did you read as a child?

As a child, from the age of 7 when I started reading, as most 7 year olds do, I began with Fairy Tales. Until 8 to 10 years, I often went to the school library to have a good choice of books. They were all fantasy ones, but at that age, I never really realized that they were fantasies, but enjoyed reading them for quite some time.

After a couple of years, I took a step off the ladder to reading comics like Little Lulu, Donald Duck, Mickey Mouse, Tom and Jerry, Dennis the Menace, Uncle Scrooge, Archies, and more.

Later around the age of 10 to 13, I went on to Enid Blyton, Nancy Drew, Roald Dahl, and more. In my later teens, I got hooked on James Hadley Chase, and read all of his books. Later I took to Sydney Sheldon thrillers, and read the complete collection of all the books there. In between, a lot more authors came in, like Somerset Maugham, Stephen King, Agatha Christie, and more.

Now it's mostly a bit of religious or relaxing books, spiritual healing books, and books to rejuvenate one...like It's never too late, or You're never too old .

What is some of the best advice your mother ever gave you?

We were eight children, and it wasn't very easy handling this big number. Dad was a very patient, kind and a non-interfering gentleman, who just went to work to feed and clothe all of us.

Mum was the one with the upper hand and controlling nature, due to the responsibilities she handled for her children. She was a total housewife, like a mother hen, taking care of her brood of chickens. One of the most important advices mum gave us was, to do well in our studies, so that someday we could all stand on our own feet without depending on our parents, our spouses, or anyone else. She said the minimum education she could give us was to complete our high school. After which we could go forward from there, and educate ourselves, as she couldn't afford to send us for further studies. Hence, each one of us chose our careers, and managed to go further after our high school.

Another advice mum gave us girls was.... not to get involved in boyfriends before finishing our high school, which would impede our performance in school. I was so naive while in school, that I followed her advice to the T and feel like I did the right thing. She also advised the boys not to indulge in smoking cigarettes, and I noticed that they all kept to her advice. During the 50's and 60's, while we were just growing up and hardly in our teens, we never really gave mum and dad any reason to hurt, or go in a wrong direction. She agreed to the partners all 8 of us chose in life belonging to our very own Anglo Indian community, and life took off from there for us

My interest in photography

www.ingramcontent.com/pod-product-compliance
Lightning Source LLC
LaVergne TN
LVHW061531070526
838199LV00010B/453